THE REALITY OF LIFE

Henk A. M. Giebels

THE REALITY

OF LIFE

Illustrations by
Chiquita M. Giebels-Wirth

GLENDALE

First published by
Glendale Publishing Ltd.
4 Haddington Tce
Dun Laoghaire
Co. Dublin

© Restor Limited, 1991
First edition 1991
New, enlarged edition 1992

British Library Cataloguing in Publication Data
A catalogue record for this book is available
from the British Library

ISBN 1–874478 04 X

Cover after a design by Anthony Maher
Cover illustration by Chiquita M. Giebels-Wirth
Origination by Wendy A. Commins, The Curragh
Printed by Colour Books, Dublin

Contents

Prologue

Dear reader,

It will become clear to you during reading that this story of God's infinite love and everlasting life is based upon factual knowledge. It is not a theory or an allegory, but as real as any material object is to everyone who sees it, although personal opinions based on the impression the object makes might differ vastly.

It is not easy to read, although I have tried to put even the deepest truth in simple words. Don't be dismayed if you do not understand everything at first. It is not a piece of fiction and like any text book it requires study. Also, what is read has to be digested, for only digested knowledge becomes wisdom and changes one's life definitively.

So therefore you should read the book more than once, slowly, a little at a time, until you come to understand the, in actual fact, very simple and beautiful reality of life, which is the infinite evolution of consciousness. Every living being is simply a soul in evolution, whether it is plant life, an animal or a human being. The outside form is only of relative importance.

Reading about a subject somewhere in the book without having read what leads up to it might make understanding much more difficult. My advice therefore is to first read the book from beginning to end without probing too deeply.

My spiritual guide is Christ and the spiritual guide of my wife Chiquita is Mary. The deeper meaning of this statement will become clear when you read 'Questions and Answers 1'. Proof of the knowledge in this book I obviously cannot give you, but remember that the highest knowledge can only come from the highest source *and that you will have to convince yourself* by careful study and pondering, so that the acquired knowledge becomes your own insight and possession which will truly change your life for the better.

I am therefore confident that this book will help you on your path of evolution.

Henk A. M. Giebels
Dublin/Ireland, March 1991
Fax: (01) 269 78 15

Spiritual Thinking

It is scientifically proven that everything consists of the same basic energy and has its own frequency. As we are limited in what we can see, anything outside our 'range' is invisible to us. But that does not mean that it does not exist!

If we raise the frequency of water, heat it up, the water becomes steam, which soon becomes invisible to us. If we cool the same steam, thus lowering its frequency, it becomes the same visible water again.

A dog-whistle gives a sound that is outside our hearing range, but can be heard by a dog.

Radio and television programmes must be chosen by their frequency, otherwise we cannot hear or see them. But we know that they exist.

Clearly then it is perfectly possible and perfectly logical, not only to imagine but also to accept, that different worlds in different frequencies can exist.

A misconception of many people is that our *body* is what and who we are, so that when our body dies *we* die. But our *real*, spiritual, self is only contained in that body, so that we can live in this physical world. Our spiritual self is of a higher frequency than our physical self and it is therefore invisible. It is the life-giving spirit that enters the body at conception and enables it to grow, and causes death when it leaves the body.

So a spirit is a person who, having no body any more through death and not yet having a new body through birth, through reincarnation, or not needing a body any more having finished his or her life-cycle on earth, is invisible. Therefore a spirit looks and acts like a human being, *is* a human being living in another world. Spirits are people.

What then is death for?

Death can be compared with a sort of sleep between two lives, a necessary sleep because we are too weak yet to withstand too many new experiences in one lifetime. Sleep softens the sharpness of the experiences of one day, so that we can handle the next day. Death has the same function between two lives — the experiences gathered can be digested in order to form part of one's personality, one's character.

People differ from each other. Of course they were all created equal by God, but with their free will they took different decisions and so developed different personalities. That is why each person starts his or her new life with the personality, character, developed in former lives.

Many people do not accept the idea of reincarnation. But consider this — how could one life be sufficient to fully develop ourselves? God would not be very just, in allowing just one lifespan, since people begin their lives in unequal conditions.

Enough for the moment.

Readers who are not as a matter of habit accustomed to spiritual thinking will now comfortably understand what follows in the next chapter.

The Author

My name is Hendrikus (usual name Henk) Anthonius Maria Giebels. I was born in 1934 in Utrecht, The Netherlands, on 20 January, the transition date between the Zodiac signs of Capricorn and Aquarius.

One particular day of my childhood which I clearly remember, was the first day of World War II. I came home from school and heard a noise in the sky. Looking up I saw aeroplanes. The war had started.

During the war I was sent away twice with some of my brothers and sisters, as our parents did not have enough food: first, half a year to a farm near Utrecht, and at the end of the war again for a further six months to a northern province.

Although the reason for being there was negative, the experiences gained by living in the countryside were positive. Milking the cows, cleaning the stables, and carrying out the other tasks assigned to me gave me a feeling for nature and animal life which was good. I still like the smell of manure!

When I was fourteen years old I was confined to bed for the greater part of a year. I had angina. I was also still growing and some-times put on one or two centimetres a week, which was an extra strain on my heart.

At the end of that year I was still weak. I had difficulty walking without falling. The doctor said I would grow out of it in time. Since I could not participate in sports I looked for compensation. I learned to play the guitar, and performed at festivals and in jazz clubs.

I was brought up a Christian.

One day when I was nineteen I heard a voice say: 'You are going to serve God'. I did not pay much attention. When the same thing happened again two weeks later I was startled. I began to wonder what this meant and then it happened for a third time, again two weeks later. Now I was frightened. I told nobody, because I did not want people to think I was imagining things. But I knew it was real, and the only thing I could think of was that God wanted me to be a priest. I prayed for weeks and then slowly calmed down. Nothing further happened. I started to forget the experience.

In the same year I finished High School.

What to do now with my life? My health was not yet what it should be.

Then the idea formed in my mind that I would start my own business. My father was willing to lend me some money. I was legally declared of age, which was necessary at that time as it was not possible otherwise to start a business under twenty-one.

The first year was a flop. I knew nothing of business and somehow had the idea that having an office, a desk and letterheads would automatically produce something. I did, however, qualify as a correspondent in the Dutch and English languages.

I had to close down my office and what little furniture I had was installed in my parents' drawing-room. I got a job in Amsterdam in an import-export company.

After three months I decided to have another go at my own business. My father provided another loan. This time I did not rent an office, but stayed at my parents' house.

I bought a number of business books and implemented everything they taught me, literally. Because I had no experience of my own I had to assume the books were right. And they were!

When I was twenty-two I was one of the largest heavy cable importers in Holland. My health had become normal. Building a business had become my hobby.

I also started selling cable handling equipment. I registered my own brand name internationally and put it on the products. This opened new markets. I started companies in Belgium and Germany. I also began to manufacture and to export worldwide.

In the meantime I had met Chiquita, born in 1935 in Indonesia. In April 1956 we met for the first time. In December that same year we married.

In 1958 our son Sjoerd was born. More than a year later our second son was born. There were problems however. After an operation he died.

In the following years Chiquita had three ectopic pregnancies. After that she could no longer have children.

As we loved children we decided to adopt one. That appeared more difficult than we had thought. When eventually we got the chance of adopting two boys of five and seven who were half-brothers, we accepted them whole-heartedly. Sjoerd was then six.

In the meantime I was experiencing health problems again. I had several check-ups, including a heart catheterisation. The diagnosis indicated a serious case of stress due to coping with too many activities. The advice of the doctors was that I leave the company for a year, without any form of contact. I had good managers, or so I thought, and wanted to be healthy again, so I followed the medical advice.

I had a holiday home built on a small island which I bought. I discovered a way to be busy doing nothing! When I returned to business after a year I felt fine again.

In business things had gone wrong. In Germany the situation was so serious that I decided to liquidate the company.

Sales in Belgium had stagnated. The sales people complained that we could not sell more without resorting to bribes, which seemed to be an accepted practice. I found that to be true. I sold the company.

I also fired the general manager of the Dutch company.

I had had some valuable lessons. Because I had more time and reason to think about life, I lost my faith. I would not say that I denied the existence of God, but if God existed He seemed like an uncaring parent, who watched with hands in pockets while the children murdered one another.

Materially I had everything one could ask for; I was even profiled in a national newspaper *De Telegraaf* as the 'Moneymaker that Started from Scratch'. Yet I was unhappy to the point that I did not want to live. Then one day something happened that influenced my life lastingly.

I went to a birthday party. The door was opened by a grey-haired heavy-set man in his sixties, who said: 'I want to speak to you, because it is my task to help you on your spiritual path.'

He had special powers he claimed and he asked me if I knew the books of a certain man who had been out of his body many times. When I said no, he advised me to read them, which I did. They described logically where we come from, where we go and what the meaning of life is. I read them again and again; for more than a year I really did nothing else. All the time I found new insights. The reality of life is of the utmost simplicity, but yet can be so very hard to comprehend. Then one day the man whom I had met at the party phoned.

'I know you read the books, Mr. Giebels. I am glad that you believe,' he said simply.

But I responded that I had no proof.

Then things started happening.

What happened first was very simple, almost crude or basic. I was watching television when I suddenly felt my left foot moving up my leg, although there was no visible or physical movement. Downwards to the point where I felt my foot had moved to, my leg was warm, but below that it had the coldness of death. I recalled the books I had read over the past year and I knew immediately that it was my spiritual foot that was moving. When I reached that conclusion it moved back and things were normal again.

On a particular Sunday morning Chiquita and I were with our three boys. All of a sudden our eldest son was stricken by a condition which left him cross-eyed. We all looked at him, dumbfounded.

Deciding to try to heal him as I had been taught in the books, I put my left hand on his eyes and his right hand in mine. When I removed my hand his eyes were normal again. This incident happened three times; after that his eyes remained normal.

I decided to help some friends who were troubled with chronic headache. Some were fearful, but those that I cured later could hardly believe that they ever had suffered headache.

One day one of my directors told me that his mother was in hospital; she feared she had cancer. Then I heard a voice saying I should cure her. I asked my colleague if it would be all right for me to pay her a visit that evening.

Later when I came home from work a voice told me to go to my study and lie down on my reclining chair. When I had done so I felt a movement in the region of my stomach and realised that a sort of cloud was entering my body through my solar plexus. As this was my first experience of this kind I was nervous, but when the 'cloud' had spread downwards and upwards throughout my body and entered my head with a sort of lightening explosion, I was really frightened.

After that it became quiet inside me and I heard the voice telling me that all was right, that there was no reason to be afraid.

I then asked if there was a spirit inside me, and the voice said, yes, that was true. We began to talk and I asked some questions to which I got very revealing answers. Then I was told to get up and go to the hospital. When I went to the kitchen, where Chiquita was preparing the evening meal, she looked at me with astonishment. Although I had felt clumsy walking with a spirit inside me, I had not realised how pale and swollen and unlike myself I looked.

At the hospital entrance my director also noticed this. We went in to his mother and talked a bit. Although I heard the voice telling me to heal her I resisted, because I did not want to make a fool of myself. When I had already stayed too long for a social visit the atmosphere became awkward. Then the urge to heal became so strong that I asked the woman to take off her glasses. At first she refused, but when I explained what I wanted to do she consented. She later told me she did this only in order to get rid of me.

The moment I placed my left hand over her eyes a current went through me, so violently that my head was thrown backwards and my body began to shake. After some time I felt a vibration like a click from her forehead in my hand and it was over. I took my hand away and asked her how she felt. She answered that she had never felt better and wanted to leave the hospital right away. Of course that was not possible, but my director told me the next morning that tests in the hospital had indicated no signs of illness any more and that she would be released after further tests later in the week.

When I came home from the hospital the spirit left me in the way it had entered.

A few weeks later I had a similar experience. As Chiquita and I had decided to move to Portugal, our summer home was for sale. In response to a newspaper advertisement I was phoned by a woman who wanted to talk to me about the house. We made an appointment for the following Tuesday at ten o'clock in the morning.

At nine o'clock that day a voice told me to first pick up a book about mental illnesses and then go to my study. Again a spirit entered my body and asked me to begin reading certain parts of the book. Just before ten o'clock I was told to get up and go to the front door. When I reached the door the bell rang. I opened the door and standing outside there were two ladies in normal dress.

I invited them in. Chiquita joined us. The ladies talked about renting the summer house, but I told them that I wished to sell, not rent, as we were leaving the country for good.

I inquired why they wanted to rent the house. To my surprise the eldest of the women answered that she was the mother superior of a mental institution, that the other woman was her assistant and that they wanted the summer house for their staff to relax in, because their work was so exhausting. She added that she did not understand why God had made life so difficult for her patients, that she had lost her faith and had made a decision to leave the institution and her order.

On hearing this I found myself explaining to her how life works, who God is, what the meaning and importance of her work was and that she should not give up. Of course it was the spirit in me who used my body to talk (Chiquita did not even recognise my voice), and I listened to what I said with the same sense of amazement the others felt. Having read about the particular subjects in advance made it easier for the spirit, because I offered no resistance as I understood what 'I' was talking about.

The sisters had questions about certain cases about which they did not know what to do, and they were so happy with and convinced by 'my' answers that they wanted to know how it was possible for me to talk the way I did. I then explained the whole situation, and they left in tears with their faith restored. It was a very beautiful and rewarding experience for Chiquita and me.

Sometimes Chiquita and I could not close our eyes in bed. When that happened we both felt a very strong urge to lie on our backs with our heads resting in a higher position than usual. Every time we tried to close our eyes they snapped open, as if connected to a spring. Then, while reclining in this position, between the hours of eleven o'clock and three in the morning our eyes were radiated upon and we experienced visions.

The first time a spirit of light materialised we were literally shaking. Imagine how I felt when I saw spirits of evil, looking like monsters and radiating a chilling cold.

A strange and touching experience was seeing souls reduced to a spark, waiting to be born again.

The first time out of my body I floated into a corner of the ceiling. I looked exactly the same as my body in bed. Floating back I fitted into my body like a hand into a glove.

On one occasion at bedtime I was attacked by a spirit of evil. It was a tremendous struggle to fight this spirit. That night I was taken out of my body and brought before three higher spirits, who gave me the motto 'Love and Simplicity'. The next day I looked ten years younger.

Once a voice told me to give a demonstration in a factory of the power of concentration. Standing either in or outside the building I found I was able with the force of 'my' concentration to stop a working machine. When I wished a machine that was out of order to operate well, I just concentrated on the broken part and thought it well, and for so long as I kept that image in my head and concentrated the machine worked.

After months of these proofs, I knew that the books were true. As Chiquita had similar experiences, I was in the privileged position that I could talk to her about everything. That was necessary in order to remain sane, for not only was it impossible to talk with people about what happened, but what I thought was meant only as proof was the beginning of something infinitely more far-reaching.

In February 1970 we went on holiday to Morocco. After checking in where we were staying we decided to walk to the town centre. On leaving the hotel I softly brushed the bannisters with my right thigh. For ten minutes I cried with pain.

During lunch I accidentally touched my thigh; it was swollen and hard as steel. After the meal I had to be carried to my room. The hotel doctor prescribed some medicine. He came every few days, but nothing helped. After two weeks I was taken to the airport, got special treatment in the plane and went straight to bed after arriving home. Our family doctor had no idea what could be wrong. He advised me to stay in bed and gave me some medicine.

Then something strange occurred. I could move without any problem or pain while I remained in bed or when I had to go to the bathroom. But the moment I wanted to leave my bed or my room for some other reason, I could not move.

I discovered that this happened to keep me still, so that over the weeks in bed a system of spiritual contact by way of physical stimuli could be developed by my spiritual guide; other forms of contact do not always work well if disturbances interfere. The system is very valuable and much more refined now. I can ask something, even during a conversation, and receive an answer right away, without people knowing. Evil spirits know about the system, but I have learned to distinguish between the good and the bad side.

Chiquita and I had plenty to think and talk about, and one of the decisions we made was to move to a sunny country. We decided to go to Algarve, the Southern province of Portugal. In August I went to have a look, bought land near the sea and rented a house in the hills. In November we moved.

Every two or three weeks I went to The Netherlands on business. After a year and a half I sold my company.

In the meantime I had designed my own house and pool. It took me two years to have them built. I bought more land around my property to rearrange my borders and sold what I did not need. All this gave me some knowledge of Algarvean real estate dealings.

When my house was completed I got bored. I became a director of a holding company in Luxembourg, which owned a venture finance company in The Netherlands. This meant a lot of travel.

We invested in the second largest real estate development in Algarve. In the course of research for this multi-million deal Chiquita and I travelled to most of the beautiful resorts around the world to see how Algarve compared. After this journey we knew that our project could compete with the best.

In April 1974, a month after the investment was in place, a revo-

21

lution broke out in Portugal. Although it was a peaceful revolution foreign residents fled and tourists stayed away. I resigned as director of the company in Luxembourg.

As I got bored again I decided to go into the real estate business, this time as a consultant. Our three sons were in The Netherlands. They had finished High School and I had wanted to give them a chance to choose for themselves where they wanted to live. Eventually all three of them came back to Portugal to assist me in expanding the business.

Over the next years my business developed into two separate companies, an estate agency and a building company specialising in villas and swimming pools.

In 1980 I was contacted by an American couple looking for a special property in order to start what they called a School of Life, a Centre for Yoga and Holistic Health. I only knew of one suitable property, my own house and land. I sold it to them and built a new house on some land I owned on the same hillside.

Over the years Chiquita and I had had many spiritual experiences, mostly positive but also negative ones, for evil spirits harassed us too. Although we were protected, we learned the hard way what life is all about. This planet is a learning place. But while good respects free will, evil does not. On the contrary, evil uses every means to destroy.

How it all works is explained from the next chapter onwards. But let me say now that good is not automatically stronger than evil. That is a dangerous idea which many well-intentioned people have. A strong good man fighting an evil weak one might easily lose, simply by being knifed in the back.

So we were trained to become more conscious, to remain alert to invisible life. Learning hurts, however, because we always wait until we are forced by pain to learn.

In the meantime I knew that I had a task in life. I had been prepared and trained from the start. I had had an encounter with a commander of a fleet of spacecraft and had witnessed what these machines could do. I had seen the coming into being of a Creation. I had been in Eternity, the All.

Although it was compelling it was hard to remain sane.

It consumed much energy.

From drinking socially I began to drink to ease tensions. Then I became very depressed. Chiquita tried to help, told me the very things I had told to other people who suffered. It made no difference. I would have taken my own life if I were not aware of the consequences. After six months I went to stay with my parents in The Netherlands for a change of environment. In the three months while I was there I slowly recovered. However, I will not forget that period. I learned that it is easier to talk than to do.

Then, in 1986, Chiquita became seriously ill. She had medical examinations in Portugal and The Netherlands. The conclusions were identical: Multiple Sclerosis. But with her spiritual knowledge she has cured herself since then. She was helped and sustained by the love and care of the School of Life on our former property. And I lectured there about the Reality of Life about which you are now going to read.

In 1990, Chiquita and I moved to Ireland, leaving our son Sjoerd in charge of the business in Portugal.

Who is God

All that exists, visible or not, had an origin. That Supreme Origin, the Supreme Soul, had the size of a bacterium and consisted of Energy. When It began to realise that It existed It began to think, which was the beginning of Consciousness. How It came into being, however, even the Supreme Origin Itself does not know.

The volume of the Energy expanded, together with Its consciousness, through Its thinking. The more the Supreme Soul developed Its consciousness the vaster Its volume became, until It was like an ocean of deep blue darkness, full of Life. For thinking energy is consciousness and that *is* Life.

That is why God wants to be known as Conscious Energy.

The name 'God' is used here, because so many people use it. It has no spatial foundation and it created, and still does, a lot of misunderstanding. In the chapter 'The Evolution of Mankind on Earth' you will read where the name comes from.

In higher spiritual worlds God is known by the name WHYTY, a name that cannot be translated but signifies 'Infinite Development of Consciousness'. It is the Spirit of God in everything, the consciousness of matter. That is why the essence of life is the development of consciousness, which gives light and is enlightenment. And as all that exists was created by God out of love, God is Consciousness and Light and Love.

The Creation of a Cosmos

Thinking leads to expression, to creation. A creative person develops ideas which he wants to express, *needs* to express, otherwise he would become frustrated. The more he develops his ideas the higher his inner tension becomes, until finally he expresses himself in an explosion of creativity.

The great example was set by the first Creator.

Initially thinking was a sort of dreaming. But to express a dream one has to develop the dream till it becomes a conscious, logical plan. To express a concrete plan one needs the will and the power of concentration, *the will-power*, to do so.

Which makes clear that the Universe is an expression of God's ideas, of His inner being, and that He created us consciously, as He is Consciousness. He thought of everything, willing it to exist, giving everything the part He wanted it to have. And His thoughts took form.

The first concrete form was the condensation of His thoughts into nebulae. After each stage of development the nebulae disappeared from sight when they spread out, rarefied; like cigarette smoke that by spreading out becomes invisible, although it is still present to the senses, particularly the sense of smell. That is the normal way in which life expands, develops. No growth process is really continuous. After each burst of creativity one has to regain forces for the next burst, otherwise the energy would not have the necessary power. A good example of this process is the human process of creating new life through intercourse. It is a constant withdrawal for new strength until the built up force results in an explosion of creativity.

That way the empty space was filled with life that would spiritualise and materialise over myriads of years.

First, after dreaming and thinking and concentrating, the nebulae became thick and dense. The spiritual body of God.

Then the Divine Energy became visible as light, for that is what growing consciousness leads to: enlightenment. In the darkness a weak light appeared and remained for some time, then disappeared. When it returned it was somewhat stronger. Over billions of years the light became stronger and stronger, but also weakened again and again, and finally space took on a shining garment of light.

So from the first darkness, the dark-blue proto-plasma, the golden light that represents God's consciousness and love was born. But also this golden light weakened again and again and slowly, through the constant change of light and darkness, other colours appeared.

In Its first stage of consciousness the Supreme Origin was mostly inspired by feeling, maternally, for feeling is feminine. But then It became more and more paternally conscious by thinking, for thinking is masculine. Creating is a combination of the two. That was the development of God's personality as Mother and Father.

Infinity was now filled with Supreme Maternal feeling and Supreme Paternal thinking from which presently new life would be born. God would split Himself!

When the built-up awe-inspiring power that looked like a fireball finally burst open in an enormous explosion, God had divided Himself into billions of light-balls, sparks, particles of His personality. This was the creation of a Cosmos, the coming into being of stars, planets and solar systems, the Macro-Cosmos.

Man did not yet exist; the Macro-Cosmos and Micro-Cosmos were still one and the same. The Macro-Cosmos would create the Micro-Cosmos when its parts, its cells, had at last attained independence. For these parts were a part of God's energy, were animated life and had to do what the Supreme Origin did: give birth, create.

As everything in space represented God, was a part of God, it had the Godly attributes of motherhood and fatherhood. Without these attributes of giving birth, creating, life could not have continued, no evolution would have been possible and life would have remained in the first stage of development.

In the next stage motherhood and fatherhood were to be represented by the moon as mother and the sun as father. If the moon had not become able to provide new degrees of animated life, no more life would have come into being and that would have been the end of Creation.

The moon as predominant force started to draw towards and into itself all life, all sparks, in its environment in the measure of the space it possessed. This process took myriads of years. There remained also billions of sparks that were further away and acquired independence. Then the moon started a long process of condensation and contraction. This way the moon became the first cosmic degree of life for this Universe.

In the centre of the moon and around it nebulae, plasma began to gather, but at first astrally, so invisible. This process continued for a long time. The nebulae became denser and denser until they were closed around the moon as a deep haze, an atmosphere. In that atmosphere the shining ball that was the moon condensed in proportion as the sun grew stronger.

For also the sun explored its environment and drew in all life in that space towards and into itself, till it became a hundred times larger than it is now. The sun became smaller by condensation and contraction, gained more consciousness and thus more light. When it began to condense, however, only a light radiation was visible.

In the meantime stars and planets came into being. What lived outside the enclosures of the moon and the sun were influenced by the radiation of the sun. At a far distance innumerable bodies were visible, all having taken a place in space and describing a fixed orbit. Every body consisted of energy and condensed.

Order reigned in this extensiveness and that order was enclosed in each body. What were once fire-balls were now planets and stars. They all had a task to fulfil. Some of them for example are concentrations of gas that are the lung system for this Universe. They see to it that the atmosphere remains pure.

Stars are celestial bodies manifesting themselves as light, although those luminous bodies have become solid masses. Their inner light irradiates, shines about the whole, like the glow-worm who sends out light and yet has a material body.

There exists more invisible energy than visible energy, however. The invisible energy is enormous in magnitude and it is that tremendous force that guides and preserves everything. It is God and means Life.

Every living being consists of energy too, for it came from the same invisible energy. Every body that is cast off, everything Man owns on Earth in material form, everything that lives in the Universe, stars, planets and those other millions of bodies, consists of energy and will one day return to its source, the Proto-Force. Nothing of all that will ever be lost. Everything will return to that Proto-Force for everything that lives will one day have fulfilled its task. Nothing exists without a purpose and nothing can exist outside God, that Conscious Energy.

The Origin of Man

The whole Divine plan of Creation is based on gradual development. Nothing came into existence overnight, everything evolved from degree to degree. The moon slowly condensed and acquired an atmosphere. Then the nebulae on the moon condensed even more and water came into existence.

The inside of the moon came to life. The moon as mother was ready to represent evolution. The inner life of the moon consisted of tiny, bulb-shaped, transparent cells, not larger than a virus. Yet they were animated life; they were an independent part of the Supreme Soul, of God.

This was only the first of millions of stages in the development of Man. The pre-embryo, the cell animated by God, would evolve in accordance with the Divine laws of Creation. The human existence had commenced.

Man would have to develop his consciousness the way God, the Supreme Soul, had developed His consciousness. For God wanted Man to be independent. He gave Man a conscience, however, consisting of the laws of creation, the set of rules by which the game of developing consciousness should be played in order not to jeopardise the harmony and balance of the whole.

Each cell began to look for another cell. The cells were predisposed to give something of themselves. That was the creative force in them, for the Supreme Origin, God, was present in all those lives. That drive was conscious animation and no life could escape from it.

Then two cells touched each other and united by suction. They were the first twin-souls, for they started eternal life together. That was the first love! Then an inner splitting took place and a new cell came into being. However, this new cell had two nuclei, melted together. When those two lives, grown together, reached a certain stage, they split. This separation happened naturally and was the end of a growth process. The two lives resulting from the split were twin-souls also. This process happened six times, so six times a pair of twin-souls created another pair of twin-souls. That is how God had planned it.

The twin-soul processes created a form of material body. Thus began the difference between the material and the spiritual body. At this point reincarnation came into existence. And from this moment on no more twin-souls were created, and new-born cells had only one nucleus, with sometimes an exception. Also from this moment on twin-souls started to go their own separate ways. Their two souls left their material cells which now acted as bodies and went to the world of the unconscious, a world attuned to the Supreme Origin. This was the beginning of the astral world. The astral world remained an empty space until the first two souls that left their bodies entered this astral world, the beginning stage of the Hereafter.

In the astral world the souls sank back into the previous stage, the Supreme Origin, and came to rest there. They went back to the source from which they had originated. The astral world was still dark, as the first souls had no consciousness yet and thus no light.

In every following stage the embryos entered the astral world with a little more spiritual energy, a little more light, as they developed into a more powerful material condition with the corresponding heightened attunement. The inner, or spiritual life in that stage followed the material life.

At first the spiritual life or souls that had left the dying cells and had gone to the astral world lived in the immediate surroundings of the material cells. Here the souls lived in a confined environment, near to the material life into which they could descend immediately. However, the more life developed the more spacious the world in which they lived became.

With each birth the material body grew stronger. At first the parents reached their material lifespan at the birth of their child, but later lived for some time after it. In the following stages they lived on for months and then years.

These lives were not yet conscious of anything, for instinct had not been born yet. But as they grew and underwent change after change the instinct awakened and they gained animal consciousness. So their first states of motherhood and fatherhood were unconscious states. Both cells were father and mother. But after every birth the cells gained some consciousness of motherhood and fatherhood.

The senses also came into being and developed. But first came feeling, which is drive and inspiration, the Supreme Origin as God in us. The centre of feeling is in the solar plexus.

Then the respiratory organs were developed, and the systems

designed to absorb material food. Then taste awakened, the feeling to know what is eaten. Then smell followed, then the light of the eyes and after that hearing.

In a later stage of development life existed in the waters and this fish stage lasted over a long period with growth of one metre, then two, three and four metres.

Slowly parts of the moon became solid and passable and life grew beyond the fish stage towards that of a seal or a sea-lion. When these creatures felt the urge to evolve further, they crawled out of the waters, laid themselves down on the shore and experienced their ending. There was an urge in them to do so. Although they had already experienced death in the waters millions of times, now they had ended their cycle on the moon and had to continue, always on a higher plane, like all of Creation.

Some people on Earth feel ashamed that they have not yet reached higher worlds. Besides the fact that some people work harder than others and advance more swiftly, there is a reason. Cells on the moon awoke from the outside to the inside by the rays of the sun. When the first cells reached the end of their cycle there, life in the centre of the moon still had to awake. The process is one of gradual development. We are where we are meant to be in that process.

The Evolution of Man

Although there were innumerable stars and planets between the primary planets of the first and second cosmic degree of life, the moon and Mars, on only a few hundred of them could human life pass over. These transition planets were necessary as gradual degrees of development; the jump from one primary planet to the other would have been too much.

The transition planets were situated outside the atmosphere of the moon, but were nourished by its radiation, like a mother radiates her inner love to her children.

The souls that had finished their life cycle on the moon had fallen asleep in the world of the unconscious, the astral world, and had come to rest there. All experiences of their lives on the moon sank deep into their inner being, reduced to their essence. Only after that process was completed were they ready to be attracted again, this time to the first transition planet of the second cosmic degree of life.

On all transition planets the development of the first stages of life was the same as that on the moon. The cells became active, touched each other, split and a new being came to life. But here that being lived somewhat longer, because here material life was animated by the already somewhat evolved souls passing over from the moon.

With time the first transition planet condensed till life was, as on the moon, the human embryo that lived in the waters, although already stronger, more animated.

Millions of years later this planet had condensed to the point that here also the human body reached the shore.

This human body had followed the path of development that life on all transition planets had to follow to develop the material body that contains the soul.

Nature was different here from that on the moon. Everything had more colour. Here too there was much water in which animal beings lived. The lower part of their bodies had already split. The ball-shaped beginning of a head was protruding and what one day would become arms and legs were now membranes.

Each following transition planet had to fulfil its part in the development of the human body. All of them received their forces from the moon, although they belonged to the second cosmic degree of life. Life on each succeeding transition planet was more evolved.

On the first two transition planets Man was already trying to move about in a human way, but this was not yet possible. On the third and fourth transition planets Man began to erect himself. He had claws and looked like a hairy animal. He achieved a lifespan of ten to twenty years; this age would grow until it reached thirty to forty years on the primary planet of the second cosmic degree of life, Mars.

With time, beings that resembled Man on Earth developed. The body slimmed down; the coarse build began to grow more refined. The inner life evolved too, although it was still not conscious. The lower part of the body neared its perfection. These beings still needed to experience further transitions, however, before they would be attracted by the primary planet of the second cosmic degree. Also here the souls had to await in the world of the unconscious again and again before being attracted.

The 'human being' at this point of his development lived in caves and under the ground to protect himself from the changes of nature. He already procreated in a human fashion. The head was already more clearly similar to Man on Earth.

In a further stage of development on a following transition planet Man began to resemble a powerful ape. He still lived in caves. The personality still had no more than animal consciousness, instinct. After a physical connection with another he continued on his way. When young lives were born no one cared for them. Man did not as yet know good or evil and lived as he innerly felt. In everything he was still unconscious. Only on the primary planet of the second cosmic degree of life, the instinct would become awakening consciousness.

Nature was different from what we experience on Earth. The waters were muddy and the lush green of plants and trees did not yet exist. What we know as normal wood substance on Earth was not yet condensed on these transition planets. Everything lived below strength, because the force of the sun was far less than it is now. The power of the present sunlight as we experience it would have transformed everything then to pulp.

Finally Man reached the primary planet of the second cosmic degree of life, Mars. Although Mars is visible from the Earth, its small transition planets are not. Moreover, like the moon, Mars has long ago fulfilled its function.

The people who lived on Mars were savage, powerful and tall, like giants. They still more resembled apes than human beings. They ate raw meat and fish, including their own kind. Fruits from giant shrubs were also eaten. Plant life was enormous in size.

These people were violent and formed groups that fought each other to the death. Weak life was killed. They were endangered by huge animals. It was a brutal life, but yet the desire to be strong and to save themselves from destruction was the beginning of the first degree of consciousness.

Were Man to have remained in his unconscious stage, good and evil would never have been conceived and the miseries thereof would not have been known. But neither would Man have been enabled to find his way back to God, to eventually become a conscious Godlike being, the purpose of Creation.

The Origin of Man on Earth

From Mars, the primary planet of the second cosmic degree of life, life passed over onto the many transition planets that led to the primary planet of the third cosmic degree of life, Earth. The first three cosmic degrees of life are situated in one solar system.

On each transition planet life started as tiny cells and developed as on the moon, the animation coming from the souls of the preceding planet. Planet after planet, life after life, the perfection of the human body took place.

The Earth and the transition planets leading to it were less condensed and hardened than Mars and its preceding planets. The astral world already lay around Earth like a haze that would condense according as the Earth became ready.

In the first stage of development of Earth enormous masses of clouds condensed to become water, and in that water life was to be seen. When material life commenced the animating life from the astral world immediately descended into the tiny cells, the way it had done on all preceding planets. The souls of the fully developed people on those other planets had returned to their first stage as Divine spark and awaited in the astral world their time to be born again on Earth. The animating life adapted itself to the physical body, in its first stage of embryonic life, the same embryo that is present in the perfect maternal body as it is now known.

What all those planets experienced the mother on Earth experiences. Man is his own creator; he received that gift from God. That is one of the reasons why a soul descends into the male *and* the female body, from the beginning of its existence on the moon onwards. For everyone has to learn to know maternal love, to experience God's miracle in all its depths, in order to evolve, to awaken spiritually.

With time, life on Earth, in the same way as on all preceding planets, developed through the fish stage to the stage of life achieved on Mars. It took myriads of years. The mother planet, the moon, was already dying, in company with many other planets that had fulfilled their task. In the same way, in about a million years from now the Earth will die, dissolve, in order to return to the invisible Energy that is God. Except on the last transition planet

34

there is no longer any developed life on the transition planets before Earth.

In the prehistoric age on Earth human beings were monstrous in size, powerful, savage and hairy. Enormously large animals also lived here. People were attacked by them and they were food for these gigantic beasts. The animals, although gentle by nature, had been attacked by Man on earlier transition planets and remembered that instinctively. They had brought their hate with them just as Man had brought his previously developed character.

With the passage of time the Earth condensed more and more. The human being slowly changed through many eras until the monstrous size had disappeared and the body had become more refined and less hairy.

The highest material degree for the human being was then the dark prehistoric body. There was as yet no white race.

There were now people living in all corners of the Earth, united in groups, forced by the animals to do so. There were species of animals also, who did not attack people even when they were attacked and killed themselves.

Groups of people attacked other groups. Groups became tribes and tribes became nations and from these nations rulers emerged. The process took a very long time, and in those millions of years many different races developed, amongst them the white race that would dominate.

People began to kill each other in mass battles. They were slaughtered by the thousands. The higher degrees of human life passed on to higher stages of feeling, but the lower degrees remained akin to the man-eaters.

White people attacked the lower degrees and, after submission by slaughter and violence, they ruled over them.

Along the way Man began to cultivate the land. The Earth went through its various eras and everything that lived on Earth changed. Everything that lived experienced both the material and at the same time the inner evolution. And there were millions of people of each of the seven degrees of body that had developed on Earth.

The highest degree is the body of the white race and the people of the Indian Subcontinent. The sixth degree is represented by the people of South East Asia, China and Japan. The fifth degree is a transition degree, spread out over the Earth, and also represented by the people of Indonesia.

The first four degrees are the black people, beginning with the bush people, who will become extinct only when there are no more people living on the last transition planet before the Earth. In each degree there are many transitions.

Scientifically these degrees seem to coincide with the many different races. In reality, however, they are the different degrees of feeling, of the inner attunement that represents the personality, the character of a person. In our Cosmos all these races only exist on Earth, for only on Earth exists the final perfection of the vehicle for the soul, the body.

In the first three degrees people were already different in build and stature from those on the last transition planet and had a belief, a feeling, that surpassed by far the belief of the highest material degrees. At first the elements of nature frightened them, but when they evolved they began to worship these powers of nature.

With their awakening consciousness people of the fourth degree began to use their free will. As a result diseases developed, because bodies were no longer instinctively treated properly. Free conscious choice led to the beginnings of good and evil, which in turn led to the cosmic learning principle of Karma, the law of cause and effect. For reincarnation first takes the soul through all seven degrees of physical development, but after that, when the physical cycle on Earth is finished, the soul is returned to any one of the last four degrees as many times as is necessary, in order to pay its debts from the past.

That is why people with a higher soul evolution, with talents and an intelligence of those of the seventh degree, might yet be in a lower physical body. This is often discernible in the leaders of a people of a lower degree, especially when they combine settling their Karma with doing something for the development of their people. Discrimination therefore is forgetting one's own past or future evolution.

The Origin of the Astral/Spiritual Worlds

With the seventh degree body, the end of physical development on Earth, all the power of evolution is at last focussed on the inner, the spiritual life of the human being. This spiritual evolution began with the making good of all the evil deeds of previous lives. Without the Divine law of cause and effect it would not have been possible to learn what must be learned in order to permanently enter the spiritual worlds. Each human being that has reached the seventh degree of physical development has accumulated an immense weight of evil deeds. Yet nobody by his or her own light alone has enough knowledge to make something of his or her life spiritually. It is through the Divine law of cause and effect, through Karma, that this knowledge is gained.

As consciousness awakened in the fourth degree of physical development, and as Man with his free will thus began to make conscious choices, in that fourth degree good and evil first came into being. So, for example, in a body of that degree the soul of a human being who had harmed or killed someone now descended; it was attracted by the soul of that person, because hate connected them. Souls began attracting souls. One life met the other life to make amends. Everyone has to experience this making amends. After a life of Karma one has to wait again in the astral world for a new body, to continue to make amends.

Until this point the astral world was the world of the unconscious, where souls rested in order to await a new body. Darkness still reigned there, for the inner human being had no light as yet. The inner *spiritual* human being had yet to be born. One could describe the word *astral* as indicating a lower spiritual stage, a stage without light, without enlightenment.

But when Man began to distinguish good and evil with his awakening consciousness, he also initiated a new world within the existing astral world. The first astral world was created by God. The second astral world was created by Man through the conscious evil he created on Earth. God had no part of this, did not want this, but knew that without his free will and consciousness Man would never be able to return to Him as a conscious Godlike being. So He chose to accept it as a product of making Man independent.

Man had been purposely created by God as a co-creator, so the more conscious he became the more he used his power of thought. Thinking controls feeling, instinct. Creation is the concentrated expression of feeling and thinking combined. In this way Man created an unseen world in the image of his hate, passion and violence: a hell. For each thought creates a form, *first in an invisible world* and then, afterwards, in a visible world. How could an object in our visible world be made, were it not first created in thought?

Therefore the outside world is the image of the inside world. Through thinking people create their own environment even to the extent that mass thinking creates the weather and nature of a region.

So if we want to change our external world, the circumstances in which we live, we must first change our internal world, the way in which we think and, as a result of that, act.

Because we are still children spiritually, we play with the awesome powers we received from God. We must first learn to accept our responsibility in the world of creation before we are fit to enter the higher worlds, the spiritual worlds, the spheres of light.

The Evolution of the Soul

The first people with an awakened consciousness who died, entered the first dark sphere and fell into a deep spiritual sleep measurable in years in earthly time. When they awoke they were conscious that they were alive. They did not know that they had died and had passed over into a spiritual world, a sphere. They wondered why it remained dark there, why there was no sun, no stars, where their family and friends were.

Before long other people passed over and entered the dark spheres also. But always only adults, for children could not live there. These people began to act as they used to act on Earth. They indulged their passions, attacked each other and killed and destroyed whatever came within their reach, just as they had done on Earth. They continued in this manner for a long time. But then slowly some began to ponder and long deeply for what they remembered of their earthly life. Suddenly they felt themselves pulled out of their condition, their darkness, by another force that was stronger than they were. A force that attracted them and brought them back to Earth, but now as astral human beings. Those astral human beings were attracted by people on Earth that had the same attunement. Thus began the phenomena of demonical possession, insanity, and evil dispositions on Earth, for the most sensitive people were possessed by these spirits, who wanted to enjoy the pleasures of earthly life again through their victims. Spiritual illness was born and will continue to plague people until there are no longer dark spheres.

The violence and passion of the possessed people on Earth now became worse, for they were reinforced by the spirits living within them. Consider how far ahead was the development of the material body at this stage from its animating life, the soul! But all this would slowly change, for the inner Man was awakening. Those spirits that returned to the Earth saw and experienced wider possibilities of indulging their passions on Earth, and exactly through this they slowly came to know other laws. For what happened? Through these ever widening experiences something in them awakened, and slowly but surely they began to see and experience, that when they did something to promote the happiness of people on Earth, to look after their welfare, there was more light. This awakening part of them made them less cold and sad. It warmed them, relieved them and enlightened them. From that moment on these spirits truly awakened. But it was not only through good deeds for others that they awakened. There was something else deep in them by which they awakened. That was the Divine spark, the Divine attunement in them that lifted them upwards, something that was awakened by themselves, because in the depth of Man is a core, a force that is his connection with and attunement to God. And then this growth weakened and faded again and once more they defected to their former life full of passion and hatred.

This process occurred over and over again. Each time they entered a higher life, they returned again and again to their former way of life. So by trial and error these spirits awakened and a long struggle between good and evil in them took place. And, slowly, some spirits emerged who only sought good, who urged people on Earth to do good, even though they themselves were not fully conscious of this.

Life on Earth continued and passed from one era into another. Although chaos still dominated, change was taking place, things were evolving spiritually, for the people who already had felt the inner warmth spread out over the Earth; as they began a higher life, life around them began to change.

Misery invariably dissolves when the individual human being awakens and in his own environment attempts to create an atmosphere in accordance with God's will. So through each good deed which Man performed on Earth and in the dark spheres, his inner life and environment changed. Light appeared in him, as his spiritual being awakened. This light became stronger and people around him noticed it. The inner Man began to feel love for all life. The more good deeds he did, the stronger his light became. The wonderful feeling of doing something for someone else made him happy. He saw through his own light how far the Earth had progressed. Now he understood the process of dying and being born again on Earth, he understood the myriad of laws enshrined in the life of the spirit. Those who had already come thus far, taught those who had not yet attained that height. Those who had already finished their cycle on Earth could now be welcomed by spirits, who brought them to the place of their destination, of their spiritual attunement.

The more beings who, having attained the highest material degree, were inwardly making something of themselves, the more people there were available to construct the spheres. The spheres of light had not yet come into being, however, for people were not yet so far advanced. First they created and traversed the twilight sphere, the sphere between the spheres of darkness and the spheres of light.

Then the first sphere of light came into being. This sphere was the exact likeness of the Earth. As the people in the spheres made spiritual progress, outward appearances became more beautiful in the same measure, not only the appearance of their own spiritual body, but also of everything around them. In this way they began to understand the spiritual laws. In the spheres also artistic feeling awakened and one art after the other was born. Material and spiritual life continued and according as time passed everything advanced, on Earth and in spiritual life. Millions of people were now contributing to the construction of the spheres of light by acting, to a greater or lesser extent, in the interest of others.

As animals were not conscious yet and thus could not live in a world without love, light, the people and their spheres had to develop to the point that they also began to see not only themselves but also animals. Those who experienced this for the first time wept with emotion. How impressive this was for them. These animals were no longer vicious; they also had experienced innumerable transition bodies and the highest species had reached spiritual attunement too. The animals would go further and higher and would follow the Divine path together with Man.

Slowly sphere after higher sphere came into being. The higher people advanced the more beautiful the spheres and their buildings, vegetation and flowers became.

Those who eventually reached the fourth sphere were totally free of the Earth. No longer did they have to return, for they had settled all their Karma, although many of them worked in the sphere of the Earth to urge Man to seek good.

Then the fifth, sixth and seventh sphere of light came into being and people passed into them. Those who had finished their task in the seventh sphere were attracted by the transition planets of another solar system, the Fourth Cosmic degree of Life. There they were born again in a material body of great refinement. Then the Fifth, Sixth and Seventh Cosmic Degrees of Life followed, after which they entered the All and had returned to God as a conscious Godlike being.

Spheres of Darkness (Hells)

The preceding chapters explain how all things originated. The last chapter describes summarily the journey of all beings and the final destination. This present chapter and the following one describe two stages in that journey and are best placed here.

Although all growth seems to be divided into seven degrees, in reality the process flows continuously, in one smooth movement. Subdivision into degrees simply makes things easier to understand. Real division in eternal life is established by one's attunement, by the level of consciousness and love one possesses.

At the end of a being's cycle on Earth that being will continue in one of the spheres. Whatever that sphere is, it will be the image of one's inner being, of one's inner level.

Someone who has indulged in much hate, passion and violence on Earth will go to the spheres of darkness, where he will be welcomed by spirits of his own attunement. The exact sphere of darkness or transition sphere thereof will depend on the depth of his evil character. There are murderers and mass murderers, people who kill and people who command to kill. There may be many different evil qualities in a character and each quality may differ in depth. But one thing is certain. People will go to a world where everybody else is of the same attunement.

Of course the degrees of will-power, of concentration, also differ, so that here too there are masters and followers, followers who are best described as slaves.

All beings in the dark spheres (where there is no love there is no light) have lived on Earth, where they were able to hide behind the masks of their bodies. Here that is not possible, here they are spiritually naked. Their outward appearance is the true reflection of their inner being. They are deformed and ugly and dressed the way they feel. The lower degrees look more like animals with clawlike hands. Whether they were rich or poor, beautiful or ugly on Earth, here they show only their spiritual attunement. In reality this is

Hell in life after death, in the Hereafter, and the people living here are usually called devils or demons on Earth.

The city in which most of them live seems on fire, because the mass aura of passion and violence flares up to the dark-brown sky like flames.

It is an endless city with bridges over streaming water and buildings decorated with scenes of disgust. For here masters in all arts and sciences live, with feelings that are well-considered and razor-sharp, but focussed only on evil. One cannot casually enter here, for these people have tremendous powers with which to dominate and destroy one's concentration. Their gaze is withering and the power of their radiation makes one suffocate.

Here nothing grows and blossoms, because there is no warmth, no love, no light. There are no children and no animals, for they cannot sink so low. (When children die, they are brought up in special spheres with loving care till they are fourteen years old. Spiritually they are of age then, because by then they have regained their attained consciousness, after which they are taken to the sphere of their attunement.)

The men and women living here possess everything they had on Earth. They have gold and silver and they wear jewels; they even have money. They live in houses and follow the high life with parties, feasts and liquor. All this is possible through their strong will and powers of concentration. Remember: thinking is creating, even more so in the spiritual worlds.

Their dress is rich and vulgar just as they are. Those who dress in rags here will soon pass over to a higher sphere, for no spirit can enter a higher sphere without first casting off the inner feelings from the lower sphere.

Here live masters of evil who provide the Earth with atrocious inventions, with the aid of thousands of helpers. They try to destroy the good on Earth in order to dominate the planet. The inventors are but instruments in their hands. They are people who use their Divine gift for evil motives, for destruction, because they desire only riches and fame.

Although these masters of evil are monsters with great powers of concentration, they too have masters, compared with whom they are like innocents, enlightened masters of evil, with a depth in attunement as high as the highest spiritual sphere. (*See* 'The Worlds of Self-Love'.)

This chapter is restricted to the evil spheres of darkness, which have many transitions beginning with the worst, where depending on their attunement people live in holes and abysses, mud and slime. People who live there crawl around or vegetate in a slumber. Their attunement has the force of a hurricane and sounds like howling. They are the people, men or women, who slaughtered thousands of their fellow men in war, but also from their quiet rooms as scientists. These people have sunk so low, that it is almost impossible for them to get on their spiritual feet again. But as God is Love, He gives them a body and a life on Earth from time to time. In those lives they are like walking dead, for their deep inner life sleeps and is not conscious. Otherwise they would cause catastrophe, for their negative powers are tremendous. They seem dumb, cannot learn and cannot be helped, for this is a spiritual condition, but slowly something changes in them and they enter the astral world again. This way they slowly climb upwards, if they want to, from transition to transition.

For people in the higher spheres of darkness reincarnation is not necessary. In those spheres there is enough action to make it possible to gain increased insight and one day go forward to a higher sphere. They may however, through the grace of God, receive another body, because in a brief life on Earth they can attain more insight than in sometimes hundreds of years in the dark spheres. On Earth they will meet souls to whom they can make amends, there is light, there is everything that makes life agreeable. In this condition it is almost impossible for them to stumble again, for they acquire much will-power. When they advance higher through the dark spheres towards the twilight sphere, they must go through all the transition stages, because in the spirit one cannot skip any part of the journey. By helping others they work on themselves.

Of course they are helped by spirits of light, when they begin to feel the awfulness of their existence and try to free themselves from it. That help is always given in love, never in pity. For pity means self-destruction. Feeling pity pushes one over into another life on a lower level, by which the helping power is lost. Pity is weakness, simply that. Pity means that one is being lived by others. Love, on the other hand, is following the road God has shown to all of us. Feeling love for life means helping the living in all conditions. But that is a struggle, a great struggle.

The Twilight Sphere

The twilight sphere lies between the spheres of darkness and the spheres of light and has many transitions. In the awakening sphere bordering on the spheres of darkness the sky is murky-grey and there is no vegetation, no blooming life. The spirits who live there are still attuned to the dark spheres and can sink back, unless they resist with all their limited powers.

The final transition sphere that borders on the first sphere of light is as a grey autumn day on Earth. Between those two border spheres lies every possible transition sphere imaginable, because they all exist on Earth.

As in other spheres all who have the same attunement are together in the twilight spheres. From all nations and religions, all ranks and classes. The poor and the rich, the learned and the illiterate from the Earth live together, because in the spiritual world only love has value.

Not all spirits come from the Earth; many come from the spheres of darkness. Those who enter here old and worn out, become younger according as they awaken spiritually, until they look only forty years old, the age that represents the attunement of this sphere. Spiritual awakening rejuvenates. In the spheres of light this process continues.

Many of the spirits coming from the Earth do not accept that they died there. They cry like children for their lost happiness.

They for instance at first believe that an illness has simply taken them out of their daily environment, to which they will return in due course.

It goes without saying that all these people receive help. There are brothers and sisters who desire to convince them of their new life. But many do not want to accept this help. They sometimes need centuries in earthly time to come to spiritual consciousness. They walk about in the misty sphere and think of all the earthly things they left behind. They feel confused and are apathetic. On Earth they learned of a Hereafter that seemed only to exist in the fantasy world of their spiritual leaders, and so they cannot accept that in reality literally everything is different. They still cry out for food and drink

47

and they regard life as dull, because there is nothing to buy, no shops, no earthly bustle and activity. Although their personality feels thirsty and hungry and wishes to enjoy a meal, in these spheres there is no need for that. These feelings and desires belong to the material world.

Often they are only convinced when they are connected with relatives who have already left the Earth. They recognise them and then slowly they have to accept the facts. Sometimes they are taken to the Earth and shown their own passing over. They cry themselves empty and long to return to the Earth right away and live their lives over again. But this is rarely possible, although, when their desire is very great, they may receive this grace from God, in which case they go to the world of the unconscious, the first astral world, and are born again.

There are also others who are happy and not at all convinced that their existence is poor. They feel nothing of the dullness and the coldness of their lives. They have a good life, so they think, and they do not desire anything else.

They do not mind that everything is bare and grey, for nature is the image of their inner attunement. The more beautiful their thinking, the more beautiful their environment would become. But as yet they do not have the necessary love.

Nor do they yet have the necessary power of concentration to lay aside their earthly clothes and their feelings of hunger, thirst and sickness. They look and feel the way they think, and they still think materially. They are limited by this. If they had achieved the ability to think of a different mode of dress with the necessary concentration, then what they presently wore would simply disappear and be substituted.

Information about all these matters is provided in the twilight spheres. The theory of spiritual life is explained, and also the true meaning of life on Earth. These lectures are given in one's own language, for in the twilight sphere people still speak their customary earthly tongue. They are not yet sufficiently conscious spiritually to understand each other by feeling. This advanced communication only begins in the first sphere of light.

Many people develop feelings of remorse and wish to make good what they did wrong. They feel unhappy and isolate themselves, because they are disgusted with their life. Then caring spirits descend, to teach them how to pass over to the next transition sphere by helping others.

When people in the twilight spheres have ascertained that they have enough love to withstand what awaits them, they descend with hundreds of their companions to the border of the dark spheres. There they divide into small units, each with a competent guide. They establish a recognition signal, for in order to enter the dark spheres they have to assume the bestial appearance of those who live there.

They make many such journeys until they are strong enough to go alone. They must gradually learn to withstand attack and develop the art of escape by concentrating on and thereby returning to their attunement.

Then one day, having worked continuously to develop their love and concentration power, they are ready to enter the spheres of light.

First a description of the sphere of the Earth is necessary at this point.

The Sphere of the Earth

The Earth is surrounded by an astral world, a sphere. In this sphere all kinds of spirits live, invisible to the human eye: spirits of light, called guardian spirits, to help and protect human beings, but also spirits of evil, to harm and destroy them.

These spirits can pass through matter without difficulty, because they have a different frequency, a different number of energy vibrations. Thus bodies of worlds of different energy vibrations can occupy the same space, or a spirit can occupy a physical body, and a material world can be penetrated and surrounded by an astral/spiritual world: just as rarefied cigarette smoke dissolves into the air and becomes invisible, although still present to the senses.

Spirits can travel with infinite speed, in a flash, for their speed depends only on their concentration power. They think of where they want to be, and depending on their power of concentration they are there instantly.

They see with spiritual eyes in a world without sunlight, for the sun belongs to the material world. Seen from the spiritual world the light of the Earth is dim. The light by which spirits see is the light they and others possess. Earthly people of good character radiate a strong bright light however poor they may be, and spiritually poor people have almost no light, no matter how rich they may be in earthly terms.

Of course, there are many rich people who possess much light. Often they have to fulfil a task on Earth, a task for which it may be important to move in certain circles or to do costly things, their money being just a tool. It should be remembered also that wealth is no guarantee against trouble or unhappiness in life, however much it may seem otherwise.

There are many demonic spirits roaming the sphere of the Earth, who interfere with spiritually unconscious human beings. In their auras they can see all of their desires. So Man himself opens the door to his soul and invites in lower beings. A demon, a low evil spirit, can enter the aura and take over the day-consciousness of a human being, if he wishes to do so. He can connect himself with one who has the same desires and character qualities he possesses.

Human beings do not realise this, because they do not feel it. But it explains why many people feel an urge to drink or use drugs more than is good for them and become addicted to the point where they are not strong enough to stop. Others are drawn strongly towards violence, to harm or kill their fellow men. The weaker they are, by character or through addiction for instance, the more vulnerable they are to invisible influences. In this way lower spirits can enjoy earthly life the way they want to, the way they were used to. Once more they can indulge in hate, passion and violence, but now through human beings. There are of course also many people on Earth of evil character, who *want* to do the evil things they do.

As already mentioned there are also many spirits of light, who want to help and protect people on Earth, or convince them of life after death. Often these are deceased loved ones or relatives, who act as guardian spirits.

Sometimes they show themselves, if it is useful or necessary to do so. To do this they must concentrate strongly on their past earthly life, otherwise they might not be recognised, for they have been rejuvenated. Although they may be remembered as old or ugly, now they may be young and beautiful in the spiritual world. As everything is concentration and strong will, their outward appearance reflects all that they innerly wish. When their body changes, so also does their clothing, their mannerisms, the sound of their voice, and so on.

Other matters relevant to this chapter will be covered by the special subjects in the second part of the book.

The Spheres of Light (The Heavens)

There are seven spheres of light, 'Heavens', with the necessary transition spheres for gradual spiritual evolution. Those living in the first sphere of real spiritual existence know where they are and that they live in Eternity, although their feelings are still material. For them the inner evolution is as important as for the human being on Earth. In both worlds the personality has to release its material feelings. There are no children here, for they live in special spheres until they have matured to an age equivalent to fourteen in earthly years. Then they are spiritually of age and have assumed their own full consciousness again.

Many people from the Earth come here thinking to meet their family, and are disappointed to discover perhaps that they live in other spheres. Sometimes they can visit each other, for the higher attunement can connect itself with the lower one. Earthly ties, however, do not necessarily have meaning in the spirit. Only bonds based on spiritual love keep their strength in the spiritual world.

The first sphere has the appearance of the Earth, although it is of spiritual substance. The sky is clouded and the wind is strong. There are flowers, trees and birds.

The spirits look like people on Earth of thirty-five to forty years old. Most of them wear garments of coarse cloth, but some are dressed with more refinement. Those will soon go to the second sphere. For the higher one goes the more beautiful one's dress becomes, as the fabric of the spiritual garment is woven from one's own thinking and feeling.

Not every spirit has the desire to work on himself, however. Many are quite content with the life and light they have and must remain for hundreds of years in the same attunement. Their development stands still and they need to be urged continuously to help others. Seeing members of their family from time to time may activate them, especially if these are further progressed and describe more beautiful lands.

But it is a battle to conquer oneself. First many pursue a study of the basic principles of the astral and spiritual worlds. Following that they go with guides in a group or privately to see in practice what they have learned. They also descend into the dark spheres, where their brothers and sisters live and need help. People who on Earth had a profession in which they cared for others, like doctors and nurses, are more amenable here and continue more rapidly.

There are houses and buildings everywhere. In the mountains, along the waterside, in the woods. Spirits may build their houses wherever they wish. These spiritual but real residences are built with the love, consciousness and taste that is the possession of the spiritual owners. It is their resting point, where they can withdraw and meditate. All these dwellings are open, so that each and every spirit can enter there. But not all spirits build houses. The spirits, for instance, who work much in the sphere of the Earth have no need of a house.

A spiritual dwelling comes into being by concentration. The radiation of the spirit condenses and forms an enclosure about him. All the qualities that form his personality create his house, erected from spiritual substance withdrawn from the Cosmos. When a spirit has sensibility towards artistic form, then his qualities in this will decorate his spiritual residence. When his personality grows and changes, his house changes accordingly. His dwelling is maintained by his concentration power, by his radiation. If he leaves it behind to move on, and withdraws his energy from it, it will have no reason or power to be and will dissolve.

There are also many large and exceptionally beautiful communal buildings set in beautiful surroundings, erected and maintained by spirits from higher spheres. These masters do this to stimulate people to advance higher, for when they see art of a higher attunement they will exert themselves that much more. This happens in every sphere. Most of these buildings are constructed of refined snow-white marble and are open on all sides, for in the spheres there is nothing to hide. All are conscious and able to feel other life. In those various temples people study assiduously. In the temple of the doctors the diseases of the Earth are studied in order to help the people on Earth. In the temple of art people work and frequently return to the sphere of the Earth to view what they created there, for all higher art on Earth is brought there by people from the spheres, in order to elevate people on Earth, to help them to become more spiritual. All great artists were first trained in the spheres, after which time they brought their art to Earth. It was their task in their life on Earth.

Most of the artists are men, for man is the creating force, whereas woman is the driving force. It is she who makes man create, it is she who is the animating force of all art. Only in the higher spheres do women actually create art.

Often art demands so much concentration that the artist is oblivious to all other life around him. Many artists therefore are prevented by their art from entering a higher sphere. For this reason the more powerful artists eventually prefer to spend their time in the dark spheres, for by helping others they grow faster and progress sooner.

When an artist from the first sphere is born again on Earth, it is of course not only to elevate Mankind, but also to make amends. For he still may have to atone for great sins and serious mistakes, even though now he possesses love and is free of hatred, passion and violence. Without this love and freedom he could not have entered the first sphere.

It is not only art of course, that is brought to Earth from the spheres. A scientist may be born there to effect an invention that is in the interest of Mankind. While on Earth these people know nothing of all this, but when they return to the spheres they can see the past and see that on Earth they reached their goal.

For, being conscious, they knew what they wished to do on Earth before they went there. Therefore these people cannot be stopped. They have a tremendous inspiration. They clear their own way, and from the spheres that way is smoothed for them. For their guiding angels, their spiritual friends and leaders, watch and help them to accomplish what they wish to do.

In the second sphere of light all appears different from the first sphere. The sky is hard blue and there are no clouds. The buildings and temples are of a more refined substance. Nature is beautiful with many flowering plants and fruit trees. The garments are more beautiful than in the first sphere and people look somewhat younger. As in all spiritual spheres the blind of the Earth can see, the deaf can hear and those who lost an arm or leg on Earth have repossessed them, because the spiritual body cannot be destroyed. To enter here one does not have to believe in God, for loving nature and all other life is the same as believing in and loving God.

Because of the constant struggle to reach the third sphere there is a certain tension in the air. For the second sphere is the transition from the first, still retaining material feelings, to the third sphere, which is purely spiritual. Here the spirits must fight their own egos, which put up a great struggle, because they are so reluctant to give up the material world. They may return to work in the dark spheres or the twilight sphere, or they might follow the route of being born again for a task on Earth.

It is also possible for these spirits to work in the sphere of the Earth, supporting and welcoming people who are dying or protecting relatives.

After the long and arduous battle which they go through to conquer the ego, to leave behind all material feelings, they then possibly enter the third sphere of light, the first truly spiritual sphere.

Here the sky is deep blue, birds of indescribable colour fly and the fruits give delicious nourishing juices. The beautiful landscape of mountains and valleys contains magnificent temples.

In various parts of the third sphere are special temples, wonderfully decorated with and surrounded by works of art, in which one can be connected with the entire Universe. This is to stimulate spirits to develop even further. These many-towered buildings rise up to the distant sky, out of sight, and are constructed of coloured marble, radiating light and open on all sides, like all spiritual dwellings.

Every sphere has temples of music and all of the other arts and sciences, and in every temple in every sphere a fountain is found, surrounded by flowers, fruits and birds. It is the heart of every building and represents wisdom, strength and love.

The third sphere is the final one to which entry is possible directly from Earth. But few people on Earth live such purely spiritual lives, or are so free from material feelings and attachments, or love every living thing so deeply, that they can enter here directly. It is the one remaining sphere in which one will still have some Karma to settle.

Between the third and the fourth sphere, which is the first spiritual sphere totally disconnected from the material world, lies a transition sphere called Summerland. Its atmosphere sparkles like a wondrous morning, its landscape is glorious with the beauty of birds and flowers and trees.

Here earthly spirits may sojourn during their sleep, when they temporarily leave their body. From their conception their spiritual body is connected to their physical body by means of an invisible and infinitely flexible life cord. If this cord were disconnected then the body would die and the spirit would never return to it.

The spirits who have temporarily left their earthly body are recognised by their dual radiation here. The added radiation is transparent and brighter than the earthling's spiritual body. They are accompanied by their guiding spirits, who protect against entities

55

attempting to sever the life cord during the journey to Summerland.

In this manner and by this means people on Earth, who need and deserve it, may meet with their loved ones already living in the spheres. They are brought together in Summerland, where they consciously enjoy each other's company. People on Earth rarely remember anything when they return to their bodies and wake up. But they feel rested and happier and sometimes they recall dreaming of a beautiful place or hearing beautiful music.

People on Earth who are chosen as mediums for spiritual work are brought to this sphere to improve their spiritual work, and so also are scientists and artists for the same purpose. These people for the most part leave their bodies unconsciously. They receive only what their leaders wish to give. Before they return to Earth they are first spiritually veiled, so that this memory will live on in their subconscious in as pure a form as possible. Not even the greatest scientist could discover anything of importance, if not helped by spirits from the spheres.

Between the third and fourth sphere also lies the highest of the two children's spheres. Those who died on Earth as unborn children or who lived up to three years before death intervened, live here. They are brought up in a Divine quietude, an environment occupied by spirits who possess true maternal love. The blue sky has a magnificent silvery glow. Here the children are taught how to love the Creator of all this beauty.

They live in complete happiness. If their parents on Earth could see how their children are cared for, they would gladly leave them in God's care. Man wants to possess his children and in his condition on Earth does not accept that one day they will be his brothers and sisters. In reality there exists only *one* mother and father: God.

The children stay in their special sphere until they are fourteen in earthly years, for evolution in the spheres, without material hindrances, requires less time than on Earth.

When children older than three years die on Earth, they go to the second of the special children's spheres between the second and third sphere of light, also until they are fourteen years old.

Most of these children are lonely for their parents. But the spiritual mother then tells the child that it has died.

For a child this is a great mystery and a great miracle, and it normally wants to know more about it. As its feeling is earthly and it must now adapt to spiritual life, it too has to study and become familiar with the spiritual laws. If an earthly bond of love was very strong the spiritual mother will go with the child, when it is ready, to the Earth, where it may see its parents and perhaps its brothers and sisters.

When children have reached the age of fourteen, and thus have regained their full consciousness and are spiritually adult, they pass over into the sphere of their attunement, where they continue their evolution.

When a mother dies, she goes to the sphere of her own attunement. Although she will never be able to live with her child, she will see it soon, if she is attuned to a higher sphere.

The fourth sphere of light is the first one where all spirits have cosmic attunement.

The fourth sphere can only be entered from the third one. It cannot be entered from the Earth except by a spirit who has already lived in the spheres of light before being born on Earth.

In the fourth sphere any comparison with the most splendid earthly environment would be poor. The sky is a radiating silvery blue. The spirits here emit a brilliant light. Their garments are like ancient Roman dresses of remarkable colours. Of all the temples here the Temple of the Soul is pre-eminent. It is built from snow-white marble that radiates light.

It stands majestically, elevated above all else. It has hundreds of towers of which the highest are no longer visible, because they are in connection with the fifth sphere. What is higher than one's own sphere always remains invisible.

This building consists of many smaller temples, each representing a sphere, from the deepest hell to the highest sphere of light. When one enters any one of these particular temples one is connected with that sphere and witnesses it. One can also be connected with Man on Earth, with planets and stars and anything in the Cosmos. One can learn all of the laws of life.

The entire Universe can be seen, all laws and enigmas can be explained. Here one can be connected with the Conscious Eternity, the All, if the masters wish it so. The Temple of the Soul is a gift from God, to show Man what he can acquire, what he can achieve if he serves and is prepared to make the supreme sacrifice. The sacrifice of his own ego.

Through the powers of the masters Man can also be connected utterly with himself. Everything from the past is recorded, even what happened thousands of centuries ago. Everything one wishes can be called back. Even the tiniest occurrence will then manifest itself and one will pass over into that reality. For, as everything is his own possession, Man needs only to pass over into his own inner life.

Therefore is written on the Temple of the Soul: 'Man, Know Yourself.'

From entering the fourth sphere hundreds of earthly years must normally elapse before one reaches the fifth sphere, where an immense radiation of silvery light shines upon everything and the landscape is of surpassing beauty.

Again there are many temples, all towering skywards. They are of varying colours and erected in different styles. All radiate an intensity of light not yet seen in the other spheres.

On a mountain enormous buildings are constructed. Hundreds of towers adorn the whole, but the highest cannot be seen, for they have a connection with the sixth sphere.

These buildings are the temples of the arts. Each of them has the familiar fountain at its heart. Huge sculptures are under construction, depicting the cycle of the soul: battle, sorrow, grief, the qualities of the character of Man. Each piece radiates its own magnificent light and colour, depending on the attunement of the scene. The materials from which the sculptures are made not only radiate light but weigh almost nothing, for they possess the gravity of the spheres, which are more and more rarefied.

Private dwellings are bulb-shaped buildings that also radiate light, the nuances of which change all the time. They are incomparable to anything on Earth. The rooms are decorated with sculptures and an abundance of flowers; everywhere are couches. These houses are erected from a spiritual substance drawn from the Cosmos and maintained by the power of love of the spirits who live in them. They are built to their desire and will radiate in accordance with the power they possess. As the spirits grow and advance even higher, everything changes accordingly. Everything lives, everything is the spirit's own life.

The heart of each house is the chamber of love, the room where again there is a fountain. From this chamber of love the spirits begin the construction of their dwelling, which ends where their powers end.

Surrounding the chamber of love are many other rooms, all representing qualities of character. There is also a room in which spirits can see their former earthly lives, for all is recorded. No thought, nothing, is ever lost.

Everywhere flowers and fruits grow, birds fly. The spirits are in contact with all life, not only with birds. For, from feeling to feeling, they can also talk with water, with a tree, with a flower.

As even the highest spirits keep on evolving by giving love, by being available for others, their houses develop together with their personalities, their character. With the growth of their character new rooms come into being. At first these additions are invisible. They can only be seen by spirits from a higher, more rarefied, sphere. But as a character quality develops a room becomes more and more visible.

The sixth sphere is more beautiful again than the fifth sphere. Its firmament is enveloped in an unimagined canopy of silver and golden light. The spirits have the appearance of twenty-five years young. They are dressed in magnificent garments that radiate in accordance with the power of their love and consciousness.

As in every sphere they have their festivities, especially musical celebrations, in temples that expand to accommodate the millions of people who enter. Here life is interpreted in music, for each being has its own symphony of evolution, of sorrow and happiness.

It might take perhaps another thousand years to enter the seventh sphere, a sphere with a golden light and a rare and breathtaking beauty. From there one is destined to go to the mental worlds, the higher cosmic degrees of life.

The Fourth Cosmic Degree of Life

When a master of the seventh sphere of light has finished his task, his evolution there, he is ready to continue his path to God. The next steps in his evolution are the mental worlds, beginning with the fourth cosmic degree of life, where his soul receives a body again. The fourth cosmic degree of life is a planetary system with its own sun, but of a much higher level or frequency than our own Universe, and therefore invisible to us human beings.

Here too are transition planets before the primary planet, each with their own attunement, for also here it would cause disturbances if a spirit from the seventh sphere of light were born directly on the primary planet. So the spirit from the seventh sphere sinks back to the stage of Divine spark in the world of the unconscious, the astral world of the mental worlds, before being born on the first transition planet. Here the splitting of the spiritual body and the soul takes place, and the soul continues its evolution.

Why a splitting of spiritual body and soul, and why enter another material world and another body again?

First our physical body was developed from the moon onwards; through that process our soul started awakening. After having achieved the perfect material body on Earth our inner life continued its development as spirit in the spheres, until it had reached the highest level of consciousness and light possible there.

To develop further a higher degree of difficulty is necessary, namely, being totally conscious *in a body*. For in the spheres it was relatively easy to use spiritual powers, since by concentration and will-power everything happened immediately and the way it was intended. But through the resistance, the restrictions, of a body, it is much more difficult to be spiritual. More concentration and will-power are then needed, and that means more mental power, more thinking and calculation and less knowing by feeling.

The splitting of spiritual body and soul means no more than that all knowledge and powers gained in the spirit sink back deep into the inner being, where they become the character, the starting point of the personality in a new life, a further evolution.

For contrary to the condition on Earth, where a spirit is *in* a body, is *not* the body, in the spheres a spirit and his body are *one*. A spiritual body is just the form of the spirit. But in the fourth cosmic degree the spirit is again *in* a body. There the body is of matter again, but matter of a much more refined nature than on Earth and comparable in its refinement with the spiritual body of the fourth sphere of light. One could say that a spirit is the personality one has developed from one's soul, and that the soul is the essence of a being. Perhaps this explanation makes a seemingly complicated and confusing set of ideas a little easier to understand, because in reality it all *is* simple.

The solar system which is the fourth cosmic degree of life, and which was created by the third cosmic degree of life, was hardly condensed when the first souls arrived in the seventh sphere of light. Here too a further explanation is useful.

Everything created by God has to evolve. Evolution is growth in consciousness and light, light being the result of consciousness. Evolution makes people and worlds more and more enlightened, at the same time as their energy level, their frequency, is raised. And that makes new worlds and the people therein invisible to each other, for each degree of development has a different frequency.

That is why and how worlds of a different frequency, of a different number of atom variations, can occupy the same space. Their atoms have so much space between one another, although all those worlds seem solid to the people living in them, that there is no obstacle to intermixing.

That is why in spatial terms, left or right, higher or lower, are almost meaningless. There is only space and that space expands. There is no beginning and no end, there is only life and all life occupies the same space. Thus the distance between the lowest hell and the highest heaven only seems interminably great for those without the necessary attunement, the necessary power. For the highest spirits traverse that distance in a flash, if they want to. It is a matter of attuning oneself to a different frequency with the necessary power of concentration.

In the same sense it is impossible to detect other Universes with earthly eyes, although they occupy the same space as our own planetary system.

Between all those different worlds there still exists the dark-blue proto-plasma that is God.

The fourth cosmic degree of life is a Universe with only seven planets on which life is born. One primary planet, hundreds of times larger than the Earth, and six transition planets situated around it. Each planet revolves around its own axis and has its own sun. The darkness of night is not really experienced, only a shadow. Less cooling is needed, for everything is more conscious than on the third cosmic degree. The planets lie closer to their suns, for their force is milder but more conscious. Because of this all life is more radiant and matter more transparent here.

There exists only one material degree of body, which has a different constitution than on Earth. The earthly body is coarse in comparison with the body here.

There are seven spiritual degrees of development, however. A spirit from the seventh sphere of light begins his development on the first transition planet, and finally reaches the highest spiritual degree on the primary planet.

Guidance to each of the planets is given centrally from the primary planet, by reincarnated masters from the All. Although they only suggest, their suggestions are always carried out.

Children are created as on Earth, but here parents know beforehand the past of a soul and where they have met. All people here are clairvoyant and clairaudient in the highest degree. They are also cosmically conscious, for as spirits in the fourth sphere of light they already achieved this. By cosmically conscious is meant that they understand their own life, the life that exists in them as their possession.

Spirits who lived together in the seventh sphere of light as twin-souls are born together in the mental worlds, although to different families. Already as children they recognise each other; they play together and grow up in the knowledge that they will always stay together. Their inner life passes over into the male and female body alternately as on Earth.

Before a man and a woman become one in order to have a child they meditate, for they know that they will receive the highest gift that God created. They know that they have to be well prepared to receive their brother or sister. When the mother feels the awakening life growing within herself, she is already connected with that life and speaks with it in the depth of her inner being. They are one in feeling and love.

When birth approaches the mother isolates and prepares herself. She listens to beautiful music that brings her into a heightened attunement and in this condition of meditation the child is born.

The child is then brought up in perfect universal love, and it loves everything that lives. It learns language and the laws of nature and science.

On the first transition planet spirits live for hundreds of years, progressing to on the primary planet thousands of years. When people die, they pass over onto the next transition planet, for one life is enough on each planet to accomplish what is intended. On Earth one has to return many times to the same stage, for people are slow to learn what has to be learned.

As people are cosmically conscious, clairvoyant and clairaudient, earthly instruments such as the telephone or television would be without purpose. If one wishes to speak to somebody else, even at a great distance, it is sufficient to attune oneself inwardly to that person and a telepathic connection exists. However, all people here speak one language; a physical language, as on Earth.

People can also manifest themselves far away from their bodies, by concentration and a strong will, and they can act and experience normally at that distance. They have developed spiritually to such an extent that they have sufficient power to split themselves, although in reality they remain one of course. They can do this not only in their own world, but also in any world or sphere in this Cosmos lower than their own attunement.

Through space they also move with inventions that would seem miracles to Man on Earth, for technically they are light years ahead of him. They are one of the peoples who visit the Earth in strange creations, so-called UFOs, although Mankind does not yet understand the meaning of these contacts. They also learn to speak the languages of the Earth.

They are vegetarian. Their refined bodies could not conceivably digest animal food.

Their art forms are so evolved that people from Earth would find them incomprehensible.

As life is material, however refined, time also exists here and people also need sleep. Life on each planet has its own attunement and everything exists in accordance with that. The fabulous beauty of people, buildings and nature is comparable with the beauty of the fourth sphere of light, although the inner Man is so much more advanced and conscious.

In the centre of the primary planet an enormous pyramid stands. In this building are instruments that make it possible to speak with masters of the All, together with other superior inventions, available to people when they are ready to receive them.

Then, one day, the people of the fourth cosmic degree of life who are sufficiently advanced, move on to even higher and more advanced solar systems.

Fifth and Sixth Cosmic Degree of Life

The fifth cosmic degree of life is a Universe with three transition planets and a primary planet, and the sixth cosmic degree of life is a Universe with one transition planet and a primary planet. The planets on which life is born have their own sun. Here too one is born into a material body, in refinement comparable with the spiritual bodies of the fifth and sixth sphere of light.

On each of the higher cosmic degrees the refined material body is virtually transparent because of the high attunement of the spirit living in it. It has already been stated in the previous chapter that on the higher cosmic degrees bodies are created and born as on Earth. However, although the origin of bodies is like that on Earth and its preceding planets, here the first cells are already perfect and from them immediately is born the perfect body, without the earthly development.

Although the bodies of people living on the fourth, fifth and sixth cosmic degrees are translucent but tangible, their leaders, masters reincarnated from the All, possess part material and part spiritual bodies. Their attunement, their frequency, is so high, that although they are reincarnated, their form is not corporeal or solid in our sense. If one touched them one would pass through them.

The beauty of environment and firmament of the fifth and sixth cosmic degrees of life can be compared to those of the fifth and sixth sphere of light.

Life in these Universes does not differ greatly from that on the fourth cosmic degree of life, although, of course, the consciousness and light, the attunement and frequency, reach far higher levels. Life on their primary planets lasts between fifteen thousand and fifty thousand earthly years.

Whereas on the fourth cosmic degree of life robots are a normal part of daily life and carry out most physical labour, on the fifth cosmic degree, in addition to this, human bodies are created from living protoplasm, just as nowadays in laboratories on Earth blood tissue, skin and real organs from live cells are grown. These beings, like the robots, perform menial tasks. They have a soul, an independent spirit, that comes from lower life forms, and like every living spirit when this soul enters a body in which it finds the right connection it further evolves spiritually. Intelligence can be stored in the brains of these creatures organically, but wisdom and spiritual growth comes only from the soul. On the sixth cosmic degree also animal forms are created.

UFOs are still in use on the fifth, but no longer on the sixth cosmic degree. Life there is so advanced spiritually that there is no further interest in this form of travel.

When the evolution of life in this Creation draws to its end the last Universe in this Cosmos is reached: the seventh cosmic degree of life.

The Seventh Cosmic Degree of Life and the All

The seventh cosmic degree of life is also a Universe, but with only one planet, with its own sun, on which life is born. Here the consciousness and love are of such a surpassing height, that this rarefied material world and its inhabitants are translucent, like the leaders of the fourth, fifth and sixth cosmic degrees of life. Leaders are no longer needed here; everyone knows his task. Life on this planet is a hundred thousand earthly years to eternally long. This whole Universe is one golden radiation. Its everlasting beauty is beyond description.

Everyone whose life on this planet has come to an end of his own volition, because he wishes to continue his evolution, falls into a deep slumber. In earthly years this sleep seems endless, but in the Cosmos time has a different meaning and in our terms really does not exist. In this sleep all experiences sink back into the deepest inner being. When the spirit as soul awakens at last it has become a Godlike Being, it is in the All, for it has become an individualised point of Energy, just like the original God was a point of Energy when He started to create and expand. The only difference is that the original God, the Supreme Origin, had no experiences then.

Now this Godlike Being may begin his own Creation, just like God as Supreme Origin did, alone or together with other Godlike Souls.

It is only necessary to abide by the laws of creation, laid down by the Originator of everything that exists.

Although each individualised spark of Conscious Energy can now initiate its own Creation, it is not obliged to do so. It may instead help the Creation it was born in, as it has limitless powers and is fully conscious of every detail of the Cosmos it lives in.

Because it has powers of the highest order it may assume any material form it wishes, for any duration. Its spiritual existence is limitless, infinite.

However, a Conscious Being in the All who has not initiated a

Creation, alone or with others, cannot yet enter the Conscious Eternity of all Cosmoses ever created and being created, for it has not yet achieved this final responsibility. It has not yet passed the ultimate test.

A Universe is a solar system and a Cosmos is the total of all solar systems of one Creation.

Origin and Evolution of Animal and Plant Life

All life evolves, whether it is animate or inanimate, because evolution is the purpose of God. Inanimate matter consists of condensed particles of the Spirit of God in everything, called WHYTY (Infinite Evolution of Consciousness), and thus has consciousness. But animal and plant life have souls, through which they grow and evolve.

The material forms of animal and plant life came into being through the decaying process of the first cells of Man that died on the moon. In this process Man relinquished part of his creative energy, from which the first animal was born. When its cell died the process repeated itself and further animal forms were born, and so on. From the lowest animal cells the first forms of plant life developed, and from there on the process continued, until plant life had reached the point where it could no longer receive a soul.

The first cell died almost immediately; the whole process of the development of life forms was more or less instantaneous. And as lower forms of life grow faster than higher ones, the first vigorous life was plant life, then animal and then Man. Higher cells give birth to lower cells, so, Man was born first. But like weeds, which grow much faster than higher plants, the lower forms became *visible* first, creating the impression that they were *born* first.

Bodies have a function in the game of Creation. They define the degrees of evolution and make them varied. Without them it would be impossible for the lower forms to develop into higher ones.

That is why it is important in what body the soul evolves. The body has to be exactly right for the next degree of evolution of the soul.

For most people it is unbelievable that a plant develops into an animal and an animal into a human being. But remember that on each planet the human cells went through many stages of development in which they behaved like animals; there was no difference.

Bodies differ only because spiritual development differs. Each being has to go through the same stages of evolution of consciousness and light and love! Every soul evolves from planet to planet through reincarnation, whether it is the soul of a plant, an animal or a human being. It is the only way of evolution, and along it many bodies become extinct when there is no need for them any more.

Plants and animals have feeling and know much more of their immediate past and future than is realised. Their feeling is still pure, because they have not yet reached the human stage of consciousness, of evil. But each does have its own character and may be sad, happy or afraid. They are often clairvoyant and clairaudient; they can see and hear frequencies not heard or seen by human beings.

Animal life developed into thousands of species. Only the higher species followed the path of human development, for the lower species developed a form of self-reproduction. After a long process of reincarnation they reach that higher stage also.

That does not mean that each animal will have to go through all the bodies that exist, for there are many parallel paths of evolution.

The attunement of the spheres of darkness is too low for animal and plant life. In the twilight sphere there is only a lower form of vegetation. But in the higher spheres animals like fishes and birds live, and also an advanced species of dog and a number of other animals.

On the fourth and fifth cosmic degrees of life there are fishes and birds also, but more evolved and beautiful. In addition there are animals that have the appearance of what we know as cows and horses, but much more refined. Milk is no longer a drink and the horselike animal is not used as a beast of burden. It may be surprising, but cows and horses are closer in attunement to the human being than dogs. Only the highest species of dog achieves the same attunement.

On the sixth cosmic degree of life there are no longer so many different animals, and like the vegetation they are of the highest attunement. They now look more like human beings.

This evolution continues until, finally, all life is ready to enter the All.

The Worlds of Self-Love

God is Conscious Energy.

Conscious Energy is generated by alternations between positive and negative, like electricity, a force of nature.

God is Love. Good, positive love, is to love others more than oneself. Evil, negative love, is to love oneself more than others. Universal love, God's love, is the balance. For God, loving all that exists is the same as loving Himself.

Increased consciousness gives increased light, for consciousness *is* light. Greater consciousness goes together with greater love for others or self-love.

In the dark spheres there is hate, passion and violence, not much consciousness. With advancing consciousness the choice between learning from one's mistakes and improving one's character, or continuing on one's path of evil, comes into being. As can be seen on Earth, not everybody repents of his wrongdoing; many people do not want to let go of the fruits of evil.

So through the choice for love of self not only the spheres of darkness, but also the worlds of enlightened evil came into being, in exactly the same way as the positive spiritual worlds had come into being through growing love for others. As the choice is a conscious one, evil will not mend its ways of itself: masters of evil enslave people and resist reform. Evil organisations on Earth show this quite clearly.

As conscious evil has light and love, its worlds know plant and animal life.

Enlightened evil is not necessarily equivalent to unhappiness, although everything in these worlds is less beautiful, because love of self alone is of a lower attunement than love for others. The difference and struggle between good and evil is eternal.

When conscious evil has reached its All its own Creation will be neutral because its self-love and the love for its Creation are equal, are in balance.

The Origin of Creations

Although a Godlike Being in the All can make a Creation on its own, it normally combines with many other Godlike Beings to do this, so long as these others followed the same path of either love for others or love for self; for these two opposites can never combine together.

A new Creation is conceived and brought into being in the same way as the Supreme Creation was created by God as Supreme Origin. As long as the laws of creation laid down by God are followed, the creators may perform their task any way they wish. That is why beings exist who never had a physical body, although when highly evolved they are free to create matter or bodies as they wish.

It is logical that Creations differ, for creating is not imitating. However, the way in which beings unite and give birth is the same for all Creations.

As the purpose of God is the evolution of consciousness, every Creation goes through spiritual growth processes that involve growing pains. That is one of the reasons why beings in other Creations are not much interested in other worlds, assuming they have developed the necessary means of communication: because they have enough problems of their own to keep them busy!

Although the number of souls in Creations may differ, the time each Creation needs to fulfil its task is more or less the same, as the beings in them have to attain the same level of consciousness. This time is more than two thousand million millions of earthly years.

After a Creation has fulfilled its task, its creators enter a slumber which lasts the same time their Creation lasted. This sleep is to let all experiences sink back and to regain forces for a new Creation.

There are always beings who remain behind in their evolution. When their creators enter their slumber and their Creation dissolves, as there is no more concentration to maintain it, every being that has not fulfilled its task to perfect itself will have to continue its evolution in another Creation.

So there is a continuous creation of one Cosmos after another, of new beings; a continuous evolution of consciousness. The Beings that create a Cosmos will always remain part of the Creations of the

Beings created by them, and so on. But *only* the first God, the Supreme Origin, is part of and remains in each and every Cosmos ever created and to be created. His Consciousness will thus grow and expand infinitely, together with the growth of consciousness of ALL Creations.

Space Travel

All exists in a different number of atom fluctuations, and travelling through space and time is based on the science of changing these frequencies.

As science on Earth is not yet capable of real space travel, of manufacturing vehicles of the kind which we call UFOs, these flying objects are from worlds with a more advanced scientific knowledge.

Besides Universes with a different frequency there also are Universes with the same one, as beings from other worlds were left behind on Earth in former times and mixed with the then rather primitive beings.

Most Universes are light years away in distance. UFOs bridge that distance in hours by dematerialising the spaceship, having first reached a tremendous speed, so that space and time are neutralised. Having cleaved through space the flying object is materialised again, and journeys of normally hundreds of years are reduced to hours. In this fashion space travellers can journey in and out of Universes.

Spiritual beings, from the spheres of light for example, do not have a material body and thus do not need vehicles to travel. But beginning with the fourth cosmic degree of life they are born again in a material body and thus are amongst those who visit us in these flying objects which we call UFOs.

To travel in time, to the past for example, spiritually or materially, is also possible.

Time is infinity subdivided into eras to make it workable. Time is relative. The higher the level of consciousness the more being is akin to doing. So time does not really exist, although chronology does.

The soul is like a jewel with many facets. In each separate life one of the facets is especially worked, till the whole jewel shines. Although the different facets seem different characters, they are not.

The past personalities continue to be part of the whole character. As a person changes (his attunement) in each life, so does his frequency. So his past lives are a part of him, within him, but in different, in varying frequencies.

A person's past also consists of the people he has had contact with.

They form one energy group. That makes it possible to go into the past and change things, for all consists of energy, the frequency of which can be altered.

As the future can be altered by changing the present, the present is affected by changing something in the past, whether it is spiritually through thinking or repenting, or materially by space travel.

The present is the further developed past, and is the past of the future a person is already creating without realising it.

Each thought and deed helps to shape that future. As this future is based on an evolving consciousness, it exists in another frequency.

Therefore people without knowing it may leave their body while sleeping and thus simultaneously live in more than one dimension, so to speak.

This explains why people with conscious out-of-body experiences often enter a world that is known, and why sensitive, mediumistic people sometimes see beings of another world, the so-called goblins or elves.

Earth evolves the same way. The present Earth is the further developed past Earth and is the past of the future Earth. Its frequency depends on the average level of consciousness of life on it.

The Evolution of Mankind on Earth

The primary planet of the third cosmic degree of life, Earth, came into being as nebulae about 646 milliards of years ago. About 46 milliards of years ago it was condensed and life commenced. Man became recognisable as such about 6 milliards of years ago.

For each form of life resting periods are necessary to regain the strength needed to evolve further. The planet Earth is also a form of life and from time to time needs rest too. It cannot rest as a whole, for that would destroy all life, so it rests partly in changing areas. These slumber periods are the ice-ages and happen every 700,000 years, with smaller glacial periods in between.

In its long history Earth has known many eras in which life evolved to high degrees of development. In those times people were capable of achieving ages of 1,000 years. But always eventually Mankind destroyed itself by terrible wars, for also in those times scientific knowledge was far ahead of spiritual development. And each time Mankind had to start anew in ignorance. In those times Earth was also used for the disposal of recidivist people from other worlds, who then mixed with the backward population of the Earth.

At other times highly evolved beings from other solar systems, who mastered space travel, descended on Earth to conquer and submit, or to help Mankind in its evolution. They were called Gods. The God from the Old Testament was such a leader.

33,000 years ago Atlantis was established between Africa and South America. At the same time the gigantic city Mu was built, far away from Atlantis in an effort to avoid war.

Although war was avoided for a long time, about 13,000 years ago power-hungry scientists from Atlantis attacked Mu with five million people and 130,000 spacecraft. With the aid of rockets scientists from Mu were able to drop a small planet on Atlantis. The resulting impact and flood wiped out Atlantis. At the same time its army destroyed Mu.

Some 25,000 years ago, to help Man with his evolution, masters from the All planned to send a Messiah. They began work on the pyramid of Gizeh. This divine monument would predict the arrival of the Christ, represent Man and express the Cosmos. As life is eternal, the pyramid never reached a complete state. Although decadence and black magic ruled much of the Earth at this time, Egypt still possessed men of great knowledge.

Then the Christ was born. He was crucified.

The evolution of Man went on. Many wars were waged. More unity between nations was seen as a need, for people lived in constant fear. Then a power-hungry dictator felt he had to bring Europe under his rule. Higher beings tried to guide his ambition, so that the resulting sorrow would awaken Man. But Man still found it easier to hate than to love and do good. Yet slowly the unity between awakening nations grew.

In 1914 World War I brought destruction and sorrow. Again technical progress meant misery for Man.

In Versailles in 1918 spiritual masters desired to use the nature of Man to try to end the constant violence, knowing that misery would prepare the defeated for the man who, full of passion, was an easy prey for evil spirits. Long ago that man had been the high priest who convinced the Jews to convict the Christ. He had a task to fulfil.

As a result World War II broke out. Masters of light made the man break with a powerful ally, for they calculated that it would destroy his power. The occupation of some nations was due to their Karma.

After the war colonisation, which had been useful for the evolution of the peoples involved, came to an end.

Now Mankind will have to evolve to the first sphere of light. It will not be easy, but it will be an enormous step forward. Compared with the present, life on Earth will be like living in paradise. The new world will be led by a reincarnated Being of Light, and war will be unknown. But Man must first go through his Karma from the past.

Special Subjects

A PERSONAL GOD

Although God is All that exists, visible and invisible, He can will a part of Himself to assume any form He wishes, in order to represent Him if necessary. In the highest world of this Creation, the seventh cosmic degree of life, He might sit around a table with Christ, Mary and other leaders, who would otherwise be invisible to each other due to their differing frequencies, to talk for instance about their strategies in their fight against Evil. Although He indeed usually assumes white hair and a beard in those circumstances, as often depicted, His face is neither old nor young, but youthful and wise.

People may therefore pray to a personal God if that makes it easier for them, as long as they know that in reality God comprises everything that exists.

PHYSICAL AND SPIRITUAL LOVE

God's love is the perfect balance of serving love and the love of self. It is the universal love for all beings, whether they are likeable or not.

All souls start their existence neutral. Alternately as man and woman they learn to know the creating and the serving side of life. In one life they have a masculine body, in another a feminine one. The intention is to acquire the combined qualities and become like God, so that they are also evenly balanced when they reach the All.

As physical attraction is the driving force of creation, sex is a pathway to God if enjoyed spiritually. It should never be harmful.

Love is the union of souls, and does not necessarily need a physical expression.

When a person receives a new body with a different sex, the old feelings may sometimes conflict with the new body. However, there is no reason why two people in the same type of body should not love each other.

If people give their love indiscriminately, it makes them vulnerable. To help others, to work with love, to create, love has to be harnessed into concentration power.

Having pity is descending to the attunement of the other party, by which the helping power is lost. It is self-destruction.

Twin-love surpasses love, the sister and brother love. This love is what one is looking for. Only when both twin-souls reach spiritual attunement will they meet in the spheres of light. On Earth they often are friends, relatives or even man and wife, but as they are in their own attunements they do not recognise each other.

When one of the two chooses a different path of love they cannot live together, although their love does not diminish. They will then only ever meet in the world of self-love or on neutral ground. For a partner to live with they choose someone in the same situation, for whom they feel a profound brother or sister love.

Twins on Earth are twin-souls. The birth of more than two children at the same time is accelerated making good.

SIN

Anything that obstructs the evolution of consciousness is against God's will and is sin. As Man needs to continue his spiritual development on Earth, cutting short his bodily life is a major sin. Sometimes an unnatural death coincides with the end of one's life term, so there is no hindering of evolution.

Unless forced by evil spirits, conscious killing means a lowering of attunement. The act of taking the life of someone with whom one has a bond of love or hate has the result that one must give that person another life through birth. If such a bond does not exist, then it suffices to give another life to anyone.

Abortion. At the moment of conception a soul, reduced to a spark, is attracted from the astral world. It enters the mother and is connected to the cell by an invisible life cord. Through this cord the soul gives life to the body. Without it there would be no growth. So abortion is wrong at any time from conception.

Suicide. If one avoids one's problems by taking one's own life, the spiritual self remains in contact with the body until that is dissolved through putrefaction or consumption by fire. After that it remains totally alone in the astral world, until what would have been its natural life term is ended. As suicide deeply hurts the soul, that person does not ever take his own life again.

A ghost often is a self-murderer who does not want to leave his old surroundings.

Killing. Practice shows that force only finds balance in force, as evil never submits voluntarily. Offering peace in these circumstances only leads to new tyranny. Evil power should be destroyed through neutral force.

Although it is a mistake to keep evil alive, if good life is endangered, wise people apply a rule of elimination by stowing evil forces away in an environment from where a return into society during life is impossible.

But killing, if unavoidable, is only right if not based on lower feelings. One must never obey orders from those who still have to learn not to kill.

Whether animal life should be killed should always be seen in the light of the place death has in God's plan of evolution.

Most human bodies are used to animal food. Even spiritual

people sometimes use animal food to reduce their physical frequency, to remain grounded.

If animals really interfere with us so that there is no choice but to do something, we might ask God to have them leave. But if they do not, we are free to remove them, even if it means extermination. It is then part of the evolution of animal life as it happens in nature. But it should be done with higher feelings, not lower.

The same applies to plant life. Part of its way to evolve is to beautify the human environment. Plants are gladly willing to serve for that, if they are handled with love.

KARMA AND FREE WILL

When Man became conscious he became responsible for his deeds, and Karma, the law of cause and effect, came into being.

For how would one know what is right, or how to avoid wrong actions in the future, if there were no consequences? As one learns from consequences one will enter a situation in which one can amend what has been done wrong, in the same or a future life. An important factor is whether the wrong deed was a conscious one and whether a bond existed.

For acquiring Karma through an unconscious deed is learning. One's spiritual attunement is not lowered by it, although the deed has to be made good. Karma acquired through a conscious action on the other hand lowers one's attunement in the process.

Undergoing Karma is positive. It means that a cosmic debt is being paid. The way a difficult situation is handled depends on one's free will and determines whether additional Karma is acquired or not.

Negative circumstances in life may give the impression that Man has no influence on life, as if life is fixed, but this is not so. He truly has a free will, which he uses through thinking and deciding. Most accidents or negative situations have nothing to do with Karma, but with wrong actions or wrong decisions in the past.

PRAYING

With a prayer one's inner being opens to the unseen. The answer depends on the attunement of the one who prays and the one prayed to. Only words without inner involvement give no result.

The best prayer is that which asks God for help, for then one's own spirit, being a part of Him, is activated. As all beings are His children God helps via others, whether they are visible or invisible; it is their way to grow.

Leave the solution of a problem to God, Who knows best. Give thanks.

In cases of Karma not too much can be done. Moreover, God's love is the love of a Parent, who is helpless if His child does not listen; it has a free will.

A good example of a prayer is:

> Dear God, All That Is. Help me to acquire Love and Simplicity, Insight and Wisdom, Strength and Courage, and let my life include the right friends, perfect development and expression of my abilities, true prosperity and soul satisfying success.

PHYSICAL AND MENTAL DISORDERS

Physical Disorders. With his free will Man often takes decisions that negatively affect his physical health; he does not use his body the proper way. Too much tension, for example, gives disturbances.

Often, when illnesses have been in the body for a long time, not even spiritual energy can cure them. Or a soul may be too strong, which causes disorders or deformities too.

Replacing negative thoughts by positive ones helps one's well-being. Repressing thoughts only makes situations worse.

Mental disturbances. When lower beings receive a new chance in life, their body is retarded through the primitive force of their soul. God knows that they otherwise would not be able to control the power of their previous lives. Psychopathy has the same cause, but here the enormous force of former lives is visible.

When lower beings manage to occupy a person's body, that person is called insane.

SPIRITUAL GIFTS

Medium. A person may serve as instrument for spirits of light, after the Karma in his lifetime has been worked out.

To serve as medium brings spiritual wisdom. In the East mediums generally become interested in learning about the proper laws governing their powers, which lead to magic.

In cases of spiritual healing, unlike the person who gives his own energy, the medium transmits the powerful energy of a spiritual master.

Inspiration is the feeling a spiritual master transmits through the solar plexus. If he wants to retain control, he works through trance.

Trance. A state in which one temporarily leaves one's body, which is then taken over by a master who uses it to teach. This happens only if a spiritual goal is served.

After an arduous training it is possible for a medium to remain conscious during trance, so that he learns more.

Aura reading. An aura is the invisible field of emanating energy of a spiritual body. In its colours the attunement of the spirit and the health of its organs can be read.

Entering a person's aura makes it easy for a spirit to influence that person's feelings.

Clairvoyance. Its value lies in the level of attunement of the spiriual guide. The images are shown to help. Higher spirits of light always give the right message, otherwise the medium himself has taken over, consciously or subconsciously.

If an instrument hears a voice outside himself, the spiritual guide is in his aura.

Psychometry. This is the sensing of the aura of a person, generally through an object. Its value depends on the attunement of the medium. Free will should always prevail.

Levitation is drawing up the inner life of an object into spiritual life, by which it loses its weight; heavy objects require the help of lower still matter-oriented spirits.

Levitation is sometimes accompanied by rapping noises. The rapping noise is caused when, through the sudden release of higher concentration, the object receives an inner shock at the moment it regains its weight.

PREDICTING

Spirits of light do not foretell the future or engage in what we call fortune telling, for that would interfere with one's spiritual development.

Their personal foretelling is a combination of clairvoyance and calculation which, together with their predominant free will, furthers the purpose of life. Also in the higher worlds one has doubts and makes mistakes.

In the case of prophesy the issue is important enough spiritually to require looking into the future to see what will happen after a certain time. This time may seem long in earthly terms, but is short in terms of the highest level from which such a prediction comes: the All. Moreover, larger scale predictions are relatively simple, as the evolution of the average attunement of people follows foreseeable lines, in which the results of free wills balance or neutralise each other.

Astrology or practical Astronomy. It is true that the day of birth indicates the character one has acquired. But this is only an indication; free will determines what one makes of one's life.

SLEEP, DREAMS AND THOUGHT-FORMS

Sleep has seven degrees of depth. Because of inner or outer disturbances many people descend no further than the third degree and easily wake up. In the third degree dreaming takes place. This is the working out of daily tensions and problems by the subconscious, the inner self. For this reason dream therapy can be useful.

It helps towards restful sleep to suggest to oneself before going to bed, to have a pleasant and joyful dream. Some dreams that are inspired and meant to teach something, wake one up.

In the fourth degree one really relaxes. There are no further disturbances and the soul receives strength through contact with higher worlds.

Death occurs in the fifth degree when the life cord is severed. In this degree it may be permitted while still connected with the invisible life cord, to leave one's body and go to Summerland, the sphere between the third and fourth spheres of light, to gain fresh strength and meet dear ones who have passed away.

The sixth and seventh degree of sleep are the degrees of coma, the state in which people are out of but in the vicinity of their body, still connected with it through their life cord. These are also the degrees through which magicians and fakirs enter other worlds consciously.

Thought-Forms. Dreams are thoughts and like thoughts they form images radiated through the skin pores into material reality in another dimension, not another world. The images dissolve when the dreaming stops, because there is no longer energy infused into them.

These thought-forms, while they last, connect with other thought-forms of the same attunement, so that dreams or thoughts, negative or positive, are reinforced. That is why negative thinking sometimes leads to actual self-destruction.

Each thought is a seed: a flower or a weed. To repent is to draw out the weed, otherwise it continues to grow and eventually will overgrow the garden.

UFOs AND EXTRATERRESTRIALS

There are many Universes with the capacity to manufacture space objects which we call UFOs. Their inhabitants are human, with a physical body, otherwise they would not need vehicles in which to travel.

The various UFOs are manned by extraterrestrials from different races with varying appearances; many of them are friendly, even the less congenial looking ones.

Many are spiritually advanced, but there are also those who are mainly only scientifically advanced.

Alliances of extraterrestrials with common interests defend space against bellicose-minded races. That is why they carry defensive weapons, because good life may not let itself destroy. Evil souls are entitled to their own evolution, so they are never destroyed unless all persuasion has failed.

The Earth has always been visited because it is one of the most beautiful planets. Now, however, with the present earthly imbalance between scientific and spiritual development, danger exists for other Universes. The extraterrestrials have to protect their own civilisations.

They will only intervene in the affairs of Earth if this is unavoidable. Although they wish to convince the Earth of their existence, they do not make more contact than necessary, for they have no desire to interfere with natural evolution.

Questions
and
Answers

Questions and Answers 1

The Holy Trinity • The Second Coming of Christ and Mary •
The Apocalypse • The End of the World • The Third Secret of
Fatima • The Last Judgment

QUESTION: Until now you did not mention Christ and Mary. Do you not attribute to them the importance they have in the Christian religion?

ANSWER: The reason is that *The Reality of Life* should not be seen solely as a Christian book, but as a book that describes the God and Life of every being, regardless of their faith.

Christ did not come on Earth to establish a Church, but to tell people about the reality of life. However, He and Mary are as important as Christian people assume they are.

QUESTION: Can you elaborate on that?

ANSWER: Yes, but only by starting from the very beginning of Creation. God namely first created only seven entities in His image and likeness to have company and co-creators for His plans. Those entities had no physical but only spiritual bodies, as exist in the spheres. They had to evolve and prove themselves like every being.

Alas, only one of them remained on God's side. We know him as the Archangel Michael.

One of the remaining six, the Archangel Lucifer (the Serpent), convinced the other five Angels that as they were equal to God in knowledge and creative power they did not need Him.

The Archangel Michael, as the only good entity, was lonely and divided himself in order to have a partner (Eve being made out of Adam). Michael and his partner are known to us as Christ and Mary. Together with God they are the highest Good Beings and together with God they form the Holy Trinity, existing of Holy Spirit. That is why the highest form is the pyramid form.

QUESTION: Are these the Jesus Christ and his mother Mary who lived in Palestine about 2000 years ago?

ANSWER: Yes and no. This question can only be adequately answered by continuing my story.

In order not to make things more confusing we shall go on calling the only two good spiritual entities of the first Creation Christ and Mary, although obviously those were not their initial names.

Christ and Mary together made a Creation of their own. Every being in their Creation remained good. Two of those beings reincarnated in the present Creation as Abraham and David to help Mankind. I say the 'present' Creation, because in between the first Creation and the one in which we now live a number of Creations have been made by the 'good' side, although slowly more and more beings in these Creations took the way of self-love, as we can see on Earth now.

The evil side, Lucifer and his followers, also made many Creations of their own, but in those Creations the majority of beings became evil, as they had not enough guidance from good beings.

Moreover, Evil grows faster than Good, because it does not respect free will. Except for God's first Creation all in all there have been 447 Creations until now, of which 100 are still in development, like the one we live in. Of the other 347 only the Seventh Cosmic Degree and the All exist and will eternally exist. However, Evil has grown so much and has become so strong cosmically that Good is in real danger of losing its eternal fight. To maintain the balance between Good and Evil God will therefore presently withdraw from all Beings in the All the power to make new Creations. Already 2000 years ago to start preparing Mankind for what is going to happen around the end of this century the spiritual entities Christ and Mary, who together comprise all Creations resulting from their first Creation, like God comprises all Creations ever made, each split off a part of their personality to have it reincarnate as Jesus of Nazareth and his mother Mary.

QUESTION: Can you say more about Jesus and his mother Mary?

ANSWER: Yes. The parts split off from the Higher Selves of Christ and Mary first had to reincarnate on the Fourth Cosmic Degree of Life, where they lived for a number of years as children, after which they reincarnated on Earth. Lowering their frequency in one transition from the All to Earth would have been too much.

Ana, an Irish woman living in Dublin, was pregnant with her first child Mary when she became a widow. She was a member of a spiritual community led by the High Priest and King of Tara and received a vision in which she was told to go to a family living near Nazareth in Palestine, where Mary was born. When Mary was twenty-one years of age Ana and Mary went back to Ireland to visit their family and the spiritual school in Dublin. There Mary became pregnant from a Higher Being who lowered his frequency for that purpose, during which union Mary was out of her body. Jesus namely needed a body that could withstand the high spiritual tensions of his task.

Ana and Mary went back to Palestine, where Mary married Joseph, who was thirty-six. After Jesus three more boys and three girls were born. One of the boys was a homosexual.

Jesus was born on 20 January in the sixth year of this era and baptised on 20 February. At baptism usually registration took place. Joseph and Mary delayed the registration to fool Herod. When Jesus was seven years old he went with Mary to Dublin for a spiritual schooling. They returned to Palestine when Jesus was ten years of age.

When Jesus was thirty-one years old the whole family went back to Dublin for a year to finish Jesus' spiritual training, which had then lasted twenty-five years. After his return to Nazareth and the start of his public life at age thirty-two he went to India, where he married an older woman who became pregnant. She stayed in India for the time being.

Jesus started his well-known public life in Palestine, during which he visited his wife from time to time. He was crucified when he was thirty-five years old on the 27th of January. Although he was thought to be dead, he recovered after three days through human and higher spiritual treatment, after which he returned with his family to his wife in India. After some years he returned to Palestine where he secretly taught, and worked as a carpenter. He travelled extensively, but never again outside Palestine, except in later years to visit his mother Mary, who went back to the spiritual community in Dublin when she was eighty and died there in a natural way when she was one hundred years old.

As a normal voyage from Ireland to Palestine at that time would take more than a year the trip sometimes was made by UFO.

Jesus had four sons and four daughters and he too died of natural causes, in Palestine, when he was 131 years of age.

The reason why things started in Ireland and were fulfilled in Palestine is that the Irish, as a people, always were and still are the most spiritual in the world, and that Palestine is the quintessential battleground of Good and Evil.

QUESTION: What about the Apocalypse, the End of the World and the Third Secret of Fatima?

ANSWER: On page seventy-nine is mentioned that Mankind now will have to evolve to the first sphere of light, the first Heaven, but that Man first must go through his Karma of the past.

Obviously there exists an overall time schedule for the evolution of Creations. At this present stage the Earth should evolve to the first positive sphere of light, to which Evil would no longer have access. Enlightened Evil knows this and puts up immense struggle to keep down this planet's attunement, established by the general attunement of the people living on it, to prevent the evolution to the first sphere. Evil is helped by the fact that democracy and the end of colonialism have set free not only the good, but also the bad people. This will lead to serious upheavals.

Although the evolution of the Earth cannot be stopped as God's will always prevails, the tensions created by this process of opposite forces will also cause natural disasters of an enormous magnitude.

All these catastrophies will reinforce the total collapse of the world economy, which in its turn will lead to the Third World War.

The first recognisable event of all this, called the Apocalypse, was the Gulf War.

Everything will happen within ten to twenty years from now and will destroy all Evil on Earth. Then at last the Earth will be free to evolve to the first sphere of light and Evil will no longer have access to it. That will mean the End of the World as it is now and the beginning of a New World of lasting peace and order. However, in accordance with their built-up Karma from the past the people of good will will have to suffer too.

The Third Secret of Fatima basically contains the above-mentioned information, with a special warning for the Catholic Church.

QUESTION: When and how will the Second Coming of Christ take place and what will His objective be? What about the Last Judgment?

ANSWER: In the Prologue is mentioned that my spiritual guide is Christ and that Mary is the spiritual guide of my wife Chiquita.

By spiritual guide is meant Higher Self. That means effectively that we are in the same position as Jesus and Mary were 2000 years ago. We also had to live some years on a higher cosmic degree, in this instance the fifth, to adapt ourselves to a much lower frequency.

My spiritual training has also taken 25 years. That is the time needed to sufficiently open up a very restraining physical body for the highest cosmic knowledge, necessary for the execution of my spiritual task. My training was often very hurtful and the reason for many physical problems. One reason was that the spiritual presence of my Higher Self in my body was raised over the years two and a half times what is normal, which also requires a body of a higher than normal frequency to start with. That is why Jesus was conceived in a special way. My task is to clarify to the world the reality of life as described in this book, so that everybody of good will knows how to live and makes the right choices in the difficult times to come. *It is their last chance* to choose the side of love instead of self-love and is therefore called the last Judgment.

What happened to me also applies to my wife Chiquita, although in a lesser degree, as her task is to support me in my work.

Although we started our earthly lives with the characters of our Higher Selves, just as everybody else starts each reincarnation with the character built up in former lives, our thoughts, decisions and actions have not always been perfect due to earthly feelings and circumstances and the fact that we only started to be aware of our spiritual task and guidance twenty-five years ago; only since about five years do we know who we really are, and that was not easy to accept. Although our Higher Selves are perfect we as human beings have to make good our wrongdoings in this lifetime also. That is the Cosmic Justice for everyone.

Of course we receive daily guidance in many ways, not only from our Higher Selves, but also from God directly, as this is a crucial moment in the evolution of His beloved children. But as any parent who loves his children He is powerless if they do not listen, for they have a free will.

Questions and Answers 2

Miracles • Organised Religion • Ghosts/Spirits • Altering Genes
•Life Sustaining Machines • Artificial Insemination • Etcetera

QUESTION: So 2000 years ago you were Jesus? Does that mean that you are going to perform miracles too?

ANSWER: When Jesus died his spiritual being regained its original frequency and became one with his Higher Self again. So what you could say is that we are a part of the same Higher Self.

Jesus himself never performed miracles. It was always God Who did them *through* him.

In the case of miracles an earthly body is too dense and confining, however much opened up by hard training, to leave the spirit in it sufficiently aware and capable of what to do and when. The Higher Self knows, but as It is at the same time represented in all existing Creations to help Evolution and the task at hand is of the utmost importance, God Himself does the miracles *if spiritually necessary and possible.*

2000 years ago it was necessary to draw attention and convince people by miracles. Nowadays there are so many would-be healers and magicians performing what look like miracles that intelligent people are not easily spiritually convinced by them. Moreover, many real miracles and apparitions are performed by Enlightened Evil to create confusion and spiritual dependency, a form of spiritual slavery, for Lucifer and his followers have the same powers Christ and Mary have.

Also, Jesus did not cure every sick person, for that is not possible. If people are ill due to Karma they may not be cured before they have paid their cosmic debt; otherwise it would harm their evolution. If they are not yet ready to change their lives spiritually it is no use curing them, for they would recreate their illness in just the same way as they got it in the first place.

At this stage of the evolution of Mankind people will have to find out what is truth and what is not by thinking, by using their intelligence. That is what the evolution of consciousness, the

104

essence of Life, is all about. So miracles through me will only happen when they further the purpose of my task, not when they would distract from it. The decision if, when and where is up to God, Who knows best.

QUESTION: What you predicted about the Apocalypse, is that really to come true?

ANSWER: I am afraid so, because that is the situation as it is at the moment, and people change only very very slowly.

People have a free will and whatever happens, that is what they decided upon. It is not only what people *do*, but especially what they *think* that matters, for that starts the creation of whatever people really want. That is why only the Holy Trinity can really foresee what will ultimately happen, as they are a part of this Creation and its people and therefore feel what people innerly have decided upon. That means that the events are certain, although the timeframe might change.

Theoretically of course anything is possible; people might totally change their thinking and behaviour, if only on the basis of the end time prediction, and that would be wonderful for it would at least postpone events and give more time for real change which could alter the outcome of the 2000 years old predictions.

QUESTION: What do you think of organised religion? Is there one religion that is better than all others?

ANSWER: The basic relationship is and should be between God and Man directly. However, Man is in evolution and has to learn from those who are further advanced, as long as he remains free to move on when he is ready for that. For also an institution like organised religion has to evolve when higher knowledge becomes available, as God and thus Life are about the infinite evolution of consciousness. Institutions consist of people, with different levels of education and wisdom and attunement; some of those people might well be evil, others might be enlightened to a very high degree.

As Man is responsible for his own evolution and has a free will, he should decide for himself by thinking and asking God for help and insight into what is best for him at the stage of life he is in. So a certain institution might be good for him at a certain stage of his evolution, but might cease to be that at another stage, in which case he should move on.

Changing one's mind is the essence of all evolution of consciousness, so nobody should ever be afraid that that would be, *could be*, against God's will.

As Man reincarnates each time in different circumstances and situations in the faith of his parents, in different lives he will have different religions. That already indicates the relative value of a certain faith.

QUESTION: What do you think of working on Sundays?

ANSWER: The Creation in seven days refers to the very first Creation. A day in that context must be seen as a cosmic day, an era. The seventh day was indeed meant to be a day of rest, of reflection and meditation to further spiritual evolution.

The main purpose of God was to set aside a certain time for higher thoughts, because without that Man was and still is inclined to forget what the real purpose of life is.

In present day circumstances Evil, which in the meantime controls the Earth, has made it very difficult for many people to keep one day a week for higher thoughts. Working on a Sunday therefore is not sinful, but should be replaced by other times set aside for meditation and reflection in the interest of Man himself.

The ultimate objective in life should of course be a state of *continuous* balance in realising what the purpose of life is and what place work has in it.

QUESTION: How is it possible that your wife Chiquita became ill with Multiple Sclerosis if she really is who you claim she is, and why was she not instantly cured by a miracle when it was established that she had it?

ANSWER: Becoming truly cosmically conscious in an earthly body requires a long and arduous training which puts a tremendous strain on mind and body. Chiquita also suffered from the effects of *my* training. As happens with every human being serious ailments are possible as a result.

Part of the training to help Mankind is to have a full understanding of other human beings' problems. Learning how to cure oneself is a part of that. It requires removing from one's inner being what led to the problem and as a result seeing that the problem, the disease in this case, dissolves, has no reason for existence any more.

QUESTION: Will people have to give away their money and material goods in order to go to heaven?

ANSWER: No, money and material goods are neutral and necessary in this life. However, what *is* important is how they are obtained and how they are handled, what is done with them.

What Jesus meant was that with a lot of money it is very easy to do wrong things and *then* it becomes very difficult to enter the higher worlds. Only in that respect being poor helps.

You have read in this book that the higher one evolves in the spiritual worlds the more beautiful life and everything in it becomes. That already indicates that spiritual improvement ultimately leads to a better, a richer life.

QUESTION: In the chapter 'The Evolution of Mankind of Earth' you mention a number of things people are generally very interested in, without going deeper to satisfy the need for more details.

ANSWER: That is done on purpose. This is a spiritual book, meant to further the evolution of Mankind, and not to distract from it by unnecessary details, like the fact that Atlantis was an evil empire with a leadership from the fifth sphere of self-love situated in what is now South Africa, that Portugal was an island at that time where Atlantic criminals were kept out of society, that Mu was situated where now the Gobi desert is, that the pyramids were built with the help of UFOs, remaining invisible to the common people, and so on.

QUESTION: Does the same apply to UFOs and extraterrestrials? For about those subjects you don't say much either.

ANSWER: Yes, indeed. Those subjects have no spiritual significance. There are many UFO bases around and on this planet, and generally speaking they protect the Earth from unfriendly spacecraft, although sometimes one of them will get through. Initially the well-known field rings were just UFO landing marks, but later on they were extended to draw the attention to the UFO existence.

UFOs and thus extraterrestrials come from different Creations and have varying appearances, just as people on Earth differ in appearance. There is nothing too special about that, except perhaps for the fact that they don't always have two eyes and that they can hugely differ in size. But then size is not very important cosmically. Look at the difference in size on Earth between an ant and an elephant, although ultimately there only exist souls in evolution in whatever form.

QUESTION: You mention that in this Creation all souls were born on the Moon, the primary planet of the first cosmic degree of life, then via transition planets went on to the primary planet of the second cosmic degree of life, Mars, after which they evolved to the primary planet of the third cosmic degree of life, the planet Earth we are living on. Do you have any proof for this theory? And is it possible to see planets of other Universes from here?

ANSWER: We indeed were born on the Moon, evolved to Mars via 175 transition planets and went on to Earth via 99 other transition planets. That this is more than a theory is proved by an article in *The European* (élan, July 26-28, 1991) called 'Meteors of Mars', in which is stated that 'Meteors from Mars have convinced scientists that there was once life on the planet'.

There are indeed outer planets from other Universes with the same frequency as ours to be seen, but not many and only with instruments. Some have human life.

QUESTION: It seems as if earthly life is real and spiritual life is not. How can we see it the way it really is?

ANSWER: By logically thinking about it. If everything came into being by (God's) thinking and so first existed in thoughtform and after that condensed into material form, the thought or spiritual worlds existed first and made the material or physical worlds.

Therefore you could say that the spheres are the thought worlds of the material worlds. To begin with the Fourth Cosmic Degree of Life both worlds are one, because people there are cosmically conscious, until the material worlds become so refined that the Seventh Cosmic Degree of Life practically exists of thoughtform. In the All everything and everyone is back at the beginning of Creation and nothing has form unless wanted.

QUESTION: People often claim to see apparitions, whether of a ghost or spirit, Christ or Mary. Are those apparitions figments of their imagination or real?

ANSWER: It will be clear from this book that there is no reason why those apparitions could not be real, although there always will be instances where people imagine things or just try to fool people for whatever reason.

Normally I myself would say 'ghost' of a spirit who is not able to leave his situation, in cases of accidental or planned suicide where Karma is involved, or because he or she does not know or accept that he passed over into the spiritual world and so prefers to stay in familiar surroundings. They can be a nuisance and frighten people, but are most of the time harmless if left alone.

It often helps to explain to them that they passed over and should move on in their own world.

Poltergeists are spirits with a mediocre spiritual attunement, who know that they passed over, but who like to tease.

Sometimes visions do not consist of real spirits or situations, but are given as help, spiritual proof, or a warning for future events, by higher spirits who have the necessary power to project such real life images.

It often occurs that a higher spirit shows him or herself and is seen as Jesus Christ or Mary. Normally they leave it that way in order not to create confusion, although sometimes Christ or Mary really project a part of their Higher Selves to appear in a human form.

QUESTION: On page twenty-eight you say that six times a pair of twin-souls created another pair of twin-souls. I don't quite understand that process.

ANSWER: I was not too clear on purpose, because I did not want to confuse you. The original pair of twin-*souls* are divided over six pairs of twin-*bodies*. Splitting spirit or a soul is quite common in Creation; it is in fact the *basis* of Creation.

Although innerly the soul always remains *one*, each of the six parts develops itself independently in order to gain more experience in a shorter time. So each soul has six personalities, living on Earth or in the spheres, only meeting each other when cosmically necessary. Innerly and outwardly they have much in common. They become one again on the Fourth Cosmic Degree of Life, the total personality having the average attunement of the six separate ones.

QUESTION: In a *Newsweek* article of July 1991 it was stated that French and American scientists have found two new clues about the journey from ape to man. May we assume that Man indeed descended from apes?

ANSWER: Yes, but there are many more roads leading to Man. There are many animals with the highest animal consciousness becoming Man with the lowest human consciousness, without it being possible to be specific as in their own kind they already can differ tremendously in consciousness.

However, it is possible to give some indication of the six basic ways Man follows in becoming human: ape (mostly orang-outang), horse, dove, seal/sea-lion, artificially made humans of the fifth cosmic degree and animals in higher worlds.

QUESTION: On page eighty-five you say something about the killing of animals in general. What do you think of killing animals for their furs, for instance, or splitting animal embryos to produce more offspring?

ANSWER: Cutting short the natural lifespan of living beings without universal love or adequate, if earthly, reasons is interfering with their natural soul evolution and thus wrong, like killing purely for moneymaking or fashion reasons. However, when killing in case of reasonable earthly necessity, it is not necessary to waste parts of the animal body like the fur.

Splitting animal embryos (an extra soul is attracted, not a twin-soul) or interfering with their genes is giving precedence to scientific development instead of natural spiritual evolution. It is not exactly a sin, but as spiritual evolution should come first, neither it is right. In deciding whether to choose this scientific path or not one, in a certain way, has to make a choice between love and self-love.

It should always be remembered that animals are *future human beings*.

QUESTION: Is it wrong to turn off a life-sustaining machine, if that machine is the only way of keeping a physical body alive?

ANSWER: No, on the contrary. Assuming that the person involved is no longer conscious and lives a vegetable life without a reasonable chance of recovery, the machine keeps the spiritual body attached to the physical body and thus prevents the natural spiritual evolution of that person.

QUESTION: May a conscious person take his own life, if he is never without pain, has no chance of recovery and does not want to live any more?

ANSWER: Only if there is no Karma involved would it not be sinful, but as one never can be sure of that it is better not to take the risk and to see the spiritual and physical agony as a tremendous opportunity for spiritual growth.

Also in this situation staying alive with the aid of machines is not spiritually necessary, because it is not a natural way, although it may provide an excellent opportunity for spiritual evolution and staying together with loved ones.

QUESTION: What do you think of artificial insemination?

ANSWER: If someone medically cannot have children it *always* has to do with Karma. As the union of two *spiritual* beings attracts and defines the new soul artificial insemination attracts the wrong soul and spiritually seen is never good.

QUESTION: Can you say something about the Karma consequences of killing in war?

ANSWER: All commanders, irrespective of their spiritual attunement, are personally responsible for their killed subordinates and have to make that good in Karma terms. If they are from higher spheres they may reincarnate and at the same time perform a task. If they do not want to reincarnate they have to make good by work from the spheres. They are *not* responsible for the killed enemy; the commanders of the enemy are.

Subordinates ordered to kill are personally responsible for every killed enemy.

So even in a just war that cannot be avoided Cosmic Justice prevails. It should force good people to think very hard about any decision involving human life.

QUESTION: What is more important in life: feeling or thinking?

ANSWER: They are equally important and should be balanced. However, what is meant here is one's own feeling and the problem on this planet is that one never can be totally sure that one's feeling is not influenced by invisible evil.

Therefore, on Earth and until the Earth has moved to the first sphere of light, thinking is more important.

QUESTION: You mention the invisible life cord several times. How is it connected?

ANSWER: It is connected from the crown of the head of the spiritual body to the solar plexus just above the stomach of the physical body.

QUESTION: Can you point out the difference between Self-love, Evil and Enlightened Evil?

ANSWER: If you choose for Self-love you are not necessarily bad, you may not really want to harm others, but when you have to choose between your own interest and the interest of other people you most of the time choose for yourself.

Evil people are bad people and don't mind harming other people to further their own interest or even for the pleasure of it.

Enlightened Evil is Evil with a high level of Consciousness and Self-love, often living in the highest cosmic worlds and the All, capable of anything to further its own interests, leaving the lower details of the execution of its plans to people or spirits with a lower attunement. That is why it is often unrecognisable as Evil until it is too late.

QUESTION: If God created Good and Evil as parts of Himself, doesn't that mean that God Himself is good *and* bad?

ANSWER: God did *not* create Evil and wants nothing to do with it. God IS and created out of pure positive Love. That so many of His beings would choose the way of self-love was something He had not foreseen at all. He had never created before, had therefore no experience and so was what we would call naive.

After He had divided Himself, each created Being having been given a free will, it was too late, for God is always true to His word whatever the outcome.

Like any normal parent God loves *all His* children, good or bad, and that love is called universal love. But He hates Evil as a force and will fight it all the way. The balance, with so much Evil in all Creations, is kept only because of the tremendous power of God, the original Creator, and the Holy Trinity. For the Holy Trinity is the first family unit consisting of pure positive Love. Christ, the name means Anointed One, is a part of God and His first real Son, and Mary, being a part of Christ, is His first real daughter. They take care of and love each other and all Good in all Creations.

That is also why the highest good force on Earth is the family unit in the smaller and wider sense, the members taking care of and loving each other, reinforcing each other's strength for the common fight against the temptations of Evil.

Symphony
of
Life

Symphony of life

Spiritual Sayings
and
Symbolic Drawings,
inspired by Mary

God is on Earth
God is everywhere
God is in everyone
God is with the sinner
and with the servant
God is Love

Christ
Son of God
not understood
not loved
dethroned
underestimated

Jesus has been received
Jesus has been crowned
Jesus has been crucified
Jesus is Master
Jesus is Love
Jesus is God's Son

The Jesus Symbol

Mary's Love for Mankind

Mary helps
to instil in people
a higher, Cosmic thinking

A man
A woman
A child
An animal
A plant
They are all a part
of God's Plan

Animals
are a part of the evolution
of Human Beings

136

People do wrong
because they do not think
of the consequences
of their deeds

~

Knowing
is being one with one's
Self

People on Earth
are like birds in the sky
knowing they received
Wisdom
Wisdom they must use

Life
is a hell
is a paradise
is a fantasy, a dream
is a Cosmic growing process
is a strife for a
Higher Power

Death
is a milestone
a Cosmic phase
that comes to everyone

Praying
is talking to God
Praying is asking God for
Force, insight and wisdom
Praying is Help

~

Wisdom
is Power
is being Master over
thoughts and spirit

Angels
are Cosmic Helpers
helping People on Earth
who ask God for Help

Evil
is a Force that refuses
to evolve

~

Children
are Human Beings still open
Cosmically to the
Symphony of Life

The World wants to be deceived
The world creates its own destruction
The world is devoid of Love
The world must become Cosmic
The world awakens, waits
prays, cries and rejoices
The world waits for the Resurrection
of the Son of God

The Universe
is like an eye waiting
for the moment to open
itself to the next phase

Karma
is the erasing of
Cosmic events

~

Evolution
is growing to the
next phase

Sins
are earthly errors
having Power over People

Sleep
is a way to
Cosmic openness to a
Higher Power

~

Peace is a Force that
goes beyond the Earth
Peace is a Force that
controls Evil

Deeds are Seeds
Deeds are displays
in good and evil
Deeds can be recognised
by their forms
of good and evil
of beautiful and ugly
Deeds of Love are Cosmic
Even deeds of Self Love

Miracles
are thoughts which People
have about God

Moon, Mars, Earth
are phases which People need
for their Evolution

~

Love
is Cosmic
It is a fountain often
misused because
Human Beings are human
beings

Loyalty
is like a diamond that
has been polished
Loyalty leads to the
opening of Cosmic powers

NOTES

NOTES

NOTES

NOTES